ETTORE MAIOTTI

The Pastel Handbook

Learning from the Masters

Clarkson N. Potter, Inc./Publishers

DISTRIBUTED BY CROWN PUBLISHERS, INC.
NEW YORK

To my wife and children

Those works not otherwise cited are those of Ettore Maiotti

English translation copyright © 1988 by Gruppo Editoriale Fabbri, S.p.A., Milan

Copyright © 1988 by Gruppo Editoriale Fabbri, S.p.A.

Copyright © 1988 by S.I.A.E. for the works of Pablo Picasso

Translated by Kerry Milis

Production Services by Studio Asterisco, Milan

Published by Clarkson N. Potter, Inc., 225 Park Avenue South, New York, New York 10003 and represented in Canada by the Canadian MANDA Group

Originally published in Italy as *Manuale pratico del pastello, del carboncino e della sanguigna*

CLARKSON N. POTTER, POTTER, and colophon are trademarks of Clarkson N. Potter, Inc.
Manufactured in Italy by Gruppo Editoriale Fabbri, S.p.A.

Library of Congress Cataloging-in-Publication Data

Maiotti, Ettore.
[Manuale pratico del pastello, del carboncino e della sanguigna. English]
The pastel handbook: learning from the Masters / by Ettore Maiotti.
Translation of: Manuale pratico del pastello, del carboncino e della sanguigna.
Includes index.
1. Pastel drawing—Technique. I. Title.
NC880.M3513 1988.
741.2'35—dc 19
ISBN 0-517-56935-3
10 9 8 7 6 5 4 3 2 1   87-3077

First American Edition

CONTENTS

INTRODUCTION

It is hard to know why and how someone becomes an artist.

Most people feel that a person is born with a natural predisposition for art, that it is a gift from nature, like the color of your eyes or the shape of your nose. After that, only you have to decide when to start using this gift. Others feel that if you are exposed to art as a child, by attending classes and visiting museums, your natural artistic talent will be brought out.

None of that happened to me. My devotion to art was the result of an error in registering for a special course in frescoes.

When I was little, I caused my parents a lot of trouble. Because I had no interest in school, the logical thing for someone with my working-class background would have been to leave school and get a job as a laborer. But since I was not a strong child, I was stuck with school.

I do not remember now whose idea it was to enroll me in the evening division of the School for Applied Industrial Arts at the Castello Sforzesco in Milan. To get into a program at the school, you had to pass an exam which consisted of drawing figures from real-life models. The day of the exam I was in a panic—I had no experience at all. Before then, the only drawings I had ever done were a few caricatures of teachers or neighbors or friends. Incredibly, though, I passed the exam and was accepted into the program.

The first two preparatory years went in a flash. I grew to like drawing more and more and threw myself into it. The third year, when we were supposed to choose a major, I went with a friend to the registrar's office to fill out the forms. I had decided to take a course of study in commercial art, and my friend was going to take fresco painting. At the last minute, he realized he had forgotten something and asked me to register for him.

I somehow also ended up in the fresco program. But destiny could not have played a better joke on me. I had excellent teachers who reinforced my interest in becoming an artist and in expressing what I felt through this medium. I tried to learn as many techniques as I could because I realized that every technique gave me another means of expression.

Lately, I have become aware that people are no longer satisfied with natural talent alone. They want technical knowledge as well. To satisfy this need, I want to make the fruits of my experience available to as many people as possible and have written a series of practical handbooks: *The Watercolor Handbook*, available in America and England, as well as books on graphics, commercial illustration, tempera, available in Europe, and now this book on pastel, charcoal, and sanguine.

In these books, I have tried to apply the same teaching methods I use with my own pupils. These mainly consist of explaining a technique very clearly, using examples when necessary, and then having everyone copy it right away. From there the students can go on, improving their technique and applying it to different subjects and themes—still lifes, the human figure, landscapes.

By starting from the very beginning and moving in steps, it is possible to reach the highest peaks.

Remember, you must always apply yourself methodically. Do not consider my advice ironclad, but see it as a set of suggestions based on years of experience, effort, and sacrifice. Never be satisfied with your first attempts. Be demanding of yourself. Study and copy the great masters of the past and the present. This is the best way to get the results you want.

Ettore Maiotti

Many different kinds of drawings can be made using charcoal, sanguine, and pastels. Charcoal or sanguine can be used alone or together; they can also be used to sketch the basic drawing for an oil painting or a watercolor. An artist working in pastels will often work with all three materials at the same time. In fact, because of their nature, they can be adapted and made part of any kind of picture. These kinds of drawings, if protected with a fixative, can last for centuries.

Charcoal

Charcoal is made from sticks of charred wood and comes in various thicknesses, from very thin sticks, used for drawing fine lines, to big fat ones, used for drawing large murals.

Pure charcoal can be found in many art supply stores. The most common sizes are sticks about $\frac{1}{4}$ inch in diameter and 5-$\frac{1}{2}$ inches long, and triangular-shaped pieces 1-$\frac{7}{8}$ inches per side and 12 inches in length.

In the past, artists used to make their own charcoal. They learned that a hard piece of wood produces a hard stick of charcoal and

a soft wood, soft charcoal. Artists first sketched with a soft piece of charcoal, which left on the paper a fine dust that could easily be brushed away. Then, after applying a fixative, the finer details were added with a harder piece of charcoal, often made from hazelnut wood. Hazelnut charcoal is no longer to be found on sale, but it has been very satisfactorily replaced by the charcoal pencil.

If, out of curiosity, you would like to try making your own charcoal, here is one way to do it.

From different kinds of trees, cut some twigs about the thickness of a pencil. The best are willow, poplar, or hazelnut—you can also use pear or cherry if you cannot find the others. Strip off the bark and gather twigs of the same wood into bundles (ten to a bundle). Tie them together with thin pieces of wire and put them in an earthenware pot, filling it completely. Seal the pot air tight with baking clay. Now place it in a hot oven set at 390° F—a wood stove or fireplace also works well. After about six hours, remove it from the fire, and when the sticks have cooled, try them out. If they break immediately, it means they were baked for too long; next time take them off

the fire sooner. If, on the other hand, they do not write at all, they must be baked a bit longer. Simply put them back in the pot, reseal it with more clay, and put the pot back on the fire.

The Charcoal Pencil

Another form of charcoal is the charcoal pencil. The pencil is made from ground black carbon and bone dust mixed with a small amount of binder, like gum arabic or gum tragacanth.

This type of charcoal is well suited to drawings in which you will also use other media, such as pastels, oils, tempera, or watercolor. When you work with this kind of charcoal, it is very important to keep the point very sharp in order to maintain a uniform line.

Because charcoal pencils are particularly good for fine detail work, they are often used to finish a drawing begun with stick charcoal.

Compressed Charcoal Chalk

Compressed charcoal chalks come in the form of square sticks that are somewhat like pure charcoal, but their pigment is quite different. Compressed charcoal chalk is made by mixing calcified bones and ground black carbon together with a binder like clay, gum arabic, or gum tragacanth. The black of this charcoal has a brownish cast, while pure charcoal, made from twigs, is bluer.

The two chalks are used in exactly the same way; the only difference besides color is erasability. Pure charcoal can be easily removed with a piece of cloth, while for compressed charcoal an actual eraser is used. Therefore you need a certain amount of skill and confidence when you draw with charcoal in order to avoid, as much as possible, erasing mistakes—otherwise your paper can get quite messy.

There is also a carbon pencil made from compressed charcoal.

Now that you know something about the different kinds of charcoal, it is time to try them out. This way you can decide for yourself which type to work with. Because each kind of charcoal is slightly different in color, each can be useful in a different way. For example, when you have to choose between two shades of black for an object in the foreground of a drawing, it is better to use compressed charcoal. This is because there is a general rule that the cooler (or bluer) colors give the illusion of a greater depth while the warmer (or redder) colors seem to bring things forward.

Sanguine Chalks and Pencils

Sanguine is found in art supply stores in the form of chalks or pencils and is made by mixing ferrous oxide in pigment form with gum arabic or gum tragacanth. The beauty of a drawing made with sanguine is unique, and even if you are working with charcoal you should certainly not overlook this medi-

um. Sanguine pencils and chalks have the same characteristics as charcoal and are used much in the same way.

If the pigment is mixed with a dry binder, it will not leave very durable marks on your paper, and the color will be easy to shade in. The color is more resistent when mixed with an oil-based binder, like wax.

Pastels

In most stores you will find two kinds of pastels available—rectangular chalks and pencils.

Pencils come in three qualities. The first has a soft, thin lead and the least durable color. The second, with a medium lead, is oilier and has a waxy binder, and the third can be used with watercolor washes.

The softest pastels are made of finely ground pigments mixed with substances like magnesium, barium, clay, etc. and then blended with a binder like gum arabic or gum tragacanth. Very soft pastels are usually considered to be the best ones; because they contain less binder, their colors are more brilliant.

Hard pastels, on the other hand, contain a high proportion of binder and can also be wax-based. This is how those familiar colored pencils are made that school children carry. One can execute an entire picture with oil pastels or use them only to give the finishing touches to a composition which was done with another medium.

Pastels used for watercolor washes offer a peculiar range of colors. They are applied just like oil pastels, but when washed over with a damp brush, their colors spread, producing the characteristic effects of a watercolor. This creates an extraordinary quality, as you will see for yourself in the following pages.

Obviously, to get best results, one should always use pastels of the highest quality.

Fixatives

Preservation is one of the most important parts of working with pastels, charcoal, and sanguine, but preservation does not necessarily mean using a fixative. For instance, many artists place their pastel drawings directly under glass and hermetically seal them. Note: This must be done very carefully as the slightest movement can smudge the surface.

The risk of ruining a drawing, while trying to preserve it, is always great, but fixative sprays are much less risky than other methods. If you follow my advice and practice, you will learn to successfully use them.

Because fixative sprays tend to make drawings darker and, with pastels, destroy some of the velvety appearance that is characteristic of the medium, fixative is best applied in steps (as we shall see later). There are excellent products available which are completely colorless and specially designed for the many different kinds of media. However, if you would like to try making your own fixative, here is a recipe.

Take damar resin and alcohol, and mix one part resin to nine parts alcohol in a container. Let this mixture sit for a few days, and then apply it with a sprayer. If your so-

lution seems too dense, add a little alcohol until it appears to be the right consistency.

Instead of resin you might try using white lacquer varnish, but then you must change the proportions to one part white lacquer varnish to twelve parts 90 percent denatured alcohol. Find a bottle or flask large enough so that, when it holds this solution, it is only half-full. Then seal the bottle and let it sit for four days, shaking it from time to time. Now, uncap the bottle, place it in a saucepan filled with boiling water, and let it simmer for about three minutes. You must be very careful when you reach this stage as the solution is highly flammable. Let the solution cool, then filter the liquid through a piece of muslin. This makes an excellent fixative for your work.

When working with these fixatives, you should always wear some kind of protective mask, and when possible, work outdoors or near an open window. Always try to avoid breathing the fumes.

Drawing Surfaces

For pastels, the best surfaces to draw on are paper, cardboard, canvas, or wood. Whichever material you choose, it should always have a somewhat rough surface.

The paper should be slightly tinted and have some "teeth" to it. Though there are many kinds of paper made especially for pastels I personally prefer a brown wrapping paper, which I use on the rough side, an inexpensive cartridge paper, or a cover stock. These kinds of papers are best for charcoal, chalks, and sanguine as well.

If the color of the paper you have is not the color you want, it can be changed by keeping the paper very taut and painting it with tempera.

Wood and canvas should be prepared with tempera. First dilute the paint with enough water to give it the consistency of olive oil, and then spread it uniformly over the surface with a wide-bristled brush. Let it dry completely and you are ready to draw.

The Work Position

As artists, we should try to follow some of the practices of the great masters of the past. Remember, discipline and tenacity bring good results.

My first suggestion is to get a solid studio easel on which you can rest drawing surfaces of different types and sizes. Mark its position on the ground with a piece of chalk,

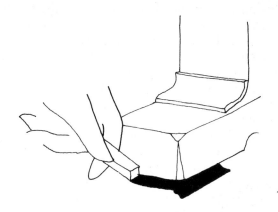

1

so that, in case you have to move it temporarily, you can find the same spot again (fig. 1).

Second, work standing up. Place your easel so you can always clearly see your subject simply by moving your head. Then position yourself directly in front of the easel (fig. 2 on p. 16).

Third, use a plumb line and a pencil to find the coordinates of your subject. For example, if you hold a plumb line with your arm stretched straight out in front of you, and you look at your subject with one eye closed, you can find all the connecting points along the vertical line formed by the plumb line (fig. 3 on p. 16).

2

You can do the same with a horizontal line by holding your pencil perfectly flat in front of you while looking at your subject with one eye closed. You will then be able to see all

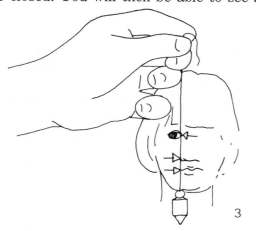

3

the points along that horizontal line (fig. 4).

As you begin to discover the structure of your subject by following its coordinates, note them on your paper. This will give you the characteristic construction lines that are

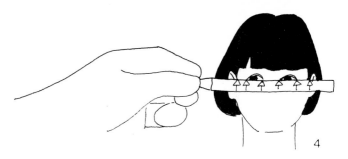

4

often found in the works of the old masters.

If you rest one hand on the paper to support yourself, try to keep a piece of absorbent paper under your hand so you do not touch the paper.

Remember that the point of a pencil reflects the skill of its owner. Of course, you can use a pencil sharpener, but a good draftsman uses a knife to shape a rapier point.

For the artist, working with a sharp pencil is as important as for an engraver working with a sharp burnisher. With a dull pencil and a dull burnisher, we would get nothing but bad drawings and inferior engravings. On a few pencils the same size as your pastels, practice shaping points with a sharp knife. Here is how to do it.

First cut down one side.

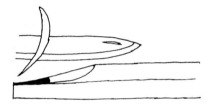

Then cut down the opposite side.

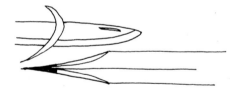

Continue to cut until you have six sides.

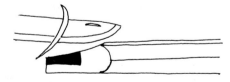

Now bevel accurately the edges of your point until you have six smooth planes.

By the time you have filled a shoe box with wood shavings, you will have acquired the ability to carry out the operation.

How to Use Pastels, Working from a Standing Position

Try to draw with your arm fully extended and straight. This way, the pencil becomes an extension of your hand. Rest the pencil point on the paper without letting your hand touch the paper. Then let your arm fall along a vertical line, as if it were weightless, dragging the pencil down the paper. This will produce a vertical line (fig. 1 on p. 18).

To draw a horizontal line, assume the same position and move your arm from left to right or right to left, as if it were the arm of a compass opening. This will give you a perfect horizontal line (fig. 2 on p. 18).

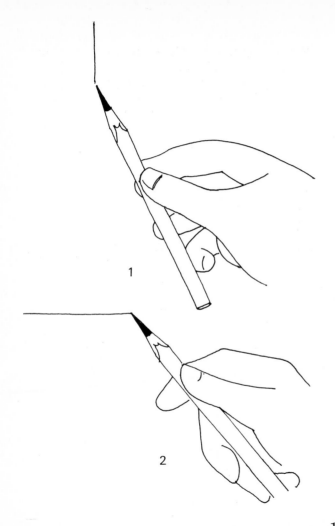

Rest your hand on the sheet as little as possible. The illustration in figure 3 shows the incorrect position.

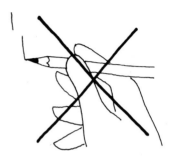

3

Maintaining the correct position is an important step in becoming a good artist. Proper training is as important for an artist as it is for a singer, a musician, or an athlete, and it can be extremely helpful to one's progress.

How to Shade with Charcoal, Sanguine, or Pastels

Once you have sketched the outlines of your subject, you must shade them in. By this, I mean you must define the areas of light and shadow.

There are various ways to do this, and each artist will choose the techniques best suited to his or her personal temperament and sensibilities.

Before trying to shade in one of your drawings, I would advise you to practice first and become familiar with the characteristics of charcoal, sanguine, and pastels.

(1) A simple quick line

(2) A line shaded with a brush

(3) A line shaded with a torchon or stump

(4) A line shaded with a piece of cloth

(5) A line shaded with a finger

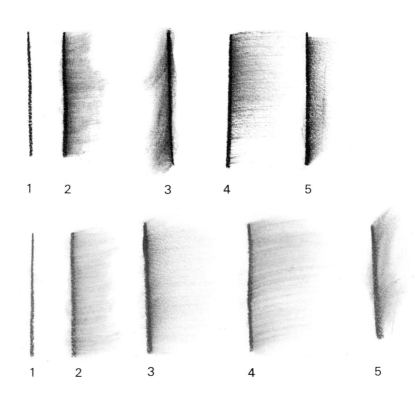

19

Cross-Hatching

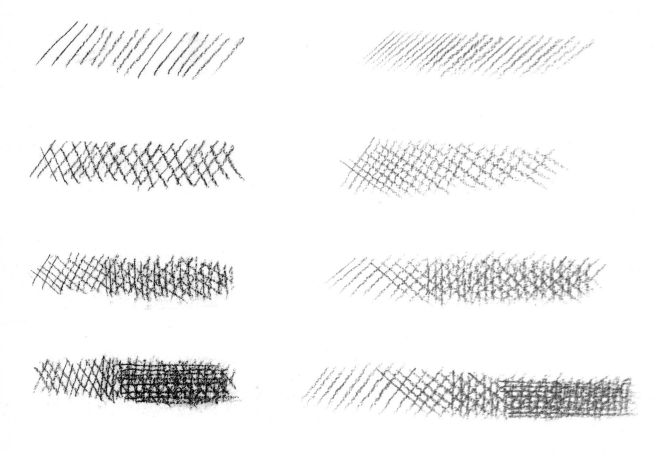

cross-hatching smudged with a brush

cross-hatching smudged with a torchon or stump

cross-hatching smudged with a cloth

cross-hatching smudged with a finger

Using Charcoal and Sanguine Chalk

Before you begin drawing with a stick of soft charcoal, a stump of compressed charcoal, or even colored chalk, it is very important for you to learn how to hold it properly (fig. 1).

If you are drawing with a round chalk, you can use any part of it to make a vertical line; but if you draw with a square chalk, it is better to use one of the sharp edges to get a clean and even line.

With your arm extended, place the full

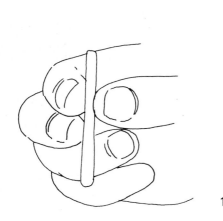

1

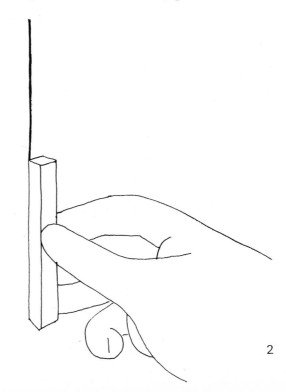

2

Depending on the effect you want, there are several ways to use charcoal and sanguine chalks. You can work with a blunt end, a flat side, or an edge.

length of the charcoal on the sheet of paper. Let your arm fall weightlessly while pressing lightly to trace a vertical line (fig. 2 on p. 22). A horizontal line is made by holding the chalk like a pencil and moving it as we described earlier, pressing with only the top edge or, with soft charcoal chalk, one end (fig. 3). In the case of square-shaped pastels, use the short side.

If you change your mind or make a mistake, you can erase it with a cloth and start again.

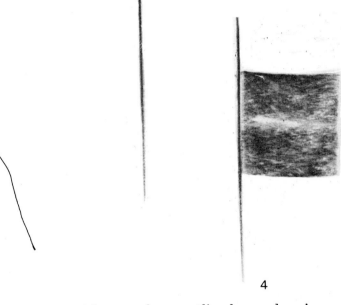

4

After you have outlined your drawing and its shadows, protect it with a thin layer of fixative.

3

Fill in the areas of halftones and full shadow, making horizontal strokes with the charcoal (fig. 4 on p. 23). Follow the same method, when you do a drawing with a charcoal pencil.

Preserve what you have just done with fixative and let it dry, then with a brush about 2 inches wide dust away the excess charcoal. This will lighten it a little, and a kind of gray halo will develop from the charcoal dust left around it.

Continue to cover your drawing with halftones, except in the area where the light falls directly. Since light areas tend to disappear under the halo produced by dusting, you may need to go back later and highlight these areas with a kneadable putty eraser.

Spray the drawing again and go over the darker areas. Hold the charcoal flat and crosshatch the shadows with vertical strokes in the opposite direction (fig. 5).

Spray it with fixative again, and when dry, dust it with your brush. Continue to cover it this way, spraying as you go along.

When you think you are done with the drawing, sharpen one end of the charcoal to a point, and go over the outlines again to give them emphasis, then spray the drawing one last time. If the light areas are not clean enough, go over them with some ordinary white chalk and do your final spraying.

Charcoal and chalks should be used on coarse, grainy paper. This can be ordinary wrapping paper turned to its rougher side, cover stock, or cartridge paper. The latter comes in white or pale straw-colored rolls from large art supply stores. Though it is not considered a very high quality paper and it is not very expensive, it does give quite good results.

5

6

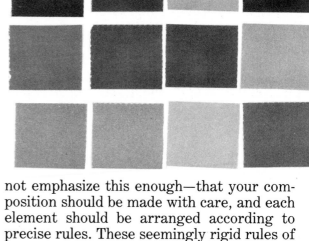

When you work with charcoal, I advise you to make larger drawings than you would with pencil. You will get aesthetically better results, and you will be more satisfied with your efforts (fig. 6 on p. 25).

The first project with charcoal pencil will be to copy a drawing, something artists of the past often did. Before we begin, however, I want to remind you—and I cannot emphasize this enough—that your composition should be made with care, and each element should be arranged according to precise rules. These seemingly rigid rules of geometry can only help your hand and eye become more coordinatated.

As you prepare the composition, keep the colors of the objects in mind. Remember to place the lighter colors in the foreground and the darker colors either in the middle distance or in the background. This rule is especially important when you are working with a single medium, whether it be charcoal or sanguine. The effect of light and shadow is created by the different tones of color.

To make this exercise easier, I have reproduced a normal color scale next to a scale of blacks. Look closely and see how the different intensities of gray correspond to the different colors on the scale.

Choose the objects in your composition carefully. Remember, that round shapes should be placed near square shapes, that the volume of light should be smaller than that of shadow, and that a light object should be smaller than a darker one.

In his *Treatise on Painting*, Leonardo da Vinci had some interesting comments on this point:

LIGHT, SHADOW, AND COLORS

The artist, who seeks glory from the ignorant masses—who only want beautiful colors—and avoids the beauty of shadows which show the marvelousness of relief in a flat object, has no understanding of the real glory of art as it is perceived by the most noble minds.

27

What is beautiful is not always good. I say this to those painters who love the beauty of color so much that they intentionally paint only weak, barely perceptible shadows, insisting that this is the right way to paint.

Shadow is a more powerful force than light for it can entirely deprive objects of light, whereas light can never chase away all the shadows of objects because these objects are solid.

An Exercise to Illustrate These Techniques

Since I was child, I have been collecting a number of ordinary objects. Each is insignificant by itself, but when they are placed next to each other, they become a source of inspiration for me because of their shape or their color.

I also like to construct geometric forms out of cardboard and cover them with chalk or white varnish. Then I arrange them in various ways to see how different sources of light affect them.

I have put some of these objects together for you to copy. I shall try to analyze my composition on the left for you, but first I will explain why I chose these pieces and why I placed them as I did.

The first task was to arrange the cloth on which the objects were placed. A plain piece of velvet works best for me because it is soft and drapes well.

I fixed the cloth to form a few angular-looking folds, then placed an old wooden box in the center of the cloth as a support for the other objects. The box gives a nice feeling of depth to the composition.

I then centered a nut-brown wooden cube in front of the box and, on the top of the box, placed a half-opened book, its cover opened toward the wall behind it. Next, I leaned a pyramid-shaped object on the book and, to the left of the cube, I placed a prism.

Against the cube, I leaned an old flask, and behind the flask, I positioned a short, squat, black bottle.

While you copy this composition, look at it closely and try to figure out its geometric construction. I have superimposed a red outline on the drawing to serve as a guide.

On the left side, as you can see, the geometric figures are arranged so that they block the movement of line from the right, almost forming a barrier.

The whole composition can fit into an imaginary rectangle.

Within the rectangle, the movement of the objects forms an irregular octagon that cre-

ates another octagon on the right side.

But the construction is not limited to this. Try to trace the axes of each element. You will see that for each vertical line, there is a horizontal line and for each diagonal line there is an opposing one.

I suggest you often repeat the exercise I have just described. When you study a drawing or a painting, look for the hidden geometric forms in its composition—especially in the works of the great masters. You will discover that nothing is left to chance; every element, every detail is calculated.

Remember that art requires dedication, practice, sacrifice, and discipline—as well as inspiration. Before learning to work with a single color, you must learn to draw. Take the most challenging courses you can find and apply yourself with great enthusiasm. This will help you train to measure up to any artistic problem with which you are faced.

In the last fifty years or so, the idea has spread that an artist does not have to follow precise rules, that figurative art should be interpretive rather than constructive. But I believe that an awareness of construction and the substance of art is somehow lost when that happens.

It is not just the masters of the past who were concerned about this. An example of the right kind of rigorousness can be found in the writings of the great Dutch abstract artist Piet Mondrian. Here is a dialogue he wrote to demonstrate the relationship between the figurative and the abstract.

LATE AFTERNOON. A PLAIN. A BOUNDLESS HORIZON. ABOVE, THE MOON.
  Y *How beautiful!*
  X *How profound the tones and colors!*
  Z *How calm!*
  Y *So nature moves you too.*
  Z *If it didn't, I wouldn't be a painter.*
  Y *Since you never portray nature, I didn't think it made any impression on you.*
  Z *On the contrary, nature moves me deeply, but I interpret it another way.*
  X *I've sometimes called your* Compositions *'symphonies', because I seem to find music in them, but not nature.*
  Z *And yet, one must see music in nature paintings as well.*
  They have their rhythm *too, even if it is not as evident as in an abstract-realist painting.*
  X *Yes, but abstract realism is expressed without reference to natural forms. It is*

similar to music, since music is not expressed through things from nature either.

Z *I don't agree with you, because the combination of sounds, at least in traditional music, expresses a certain* form *which, even if not* visible, *is always* audible. *What you can hear can be quite naturalistic, traditional music teaches us that! And then I do see an analogy between abstract-realist painting and modern music, where melody and formal structure have been abolished. But this isn't what you mean. You want to separate abstract realism from natural painting, but a separation between two expressions of the same art doesn't exist, in the sense that the latter would go beyond the realm of the art of painting. As diverse as they are in* appearance, *there is no substantial difference between these two expressions of art. Let's go back to the origins of the work of art:* our emotions when confronted with beauty. *Is the emotion we feel the same in each of us at first? Do you remember our reactions when we saw the landscape? We were all taken by its* beauty, *but you mentioned its* colors *and* tone *while I noted the calm suggested by the beauty of its colors and tone.*

(From M. Seuphor and P. Mondrian, *Leben und Werk*, Dumont, Köln 1956.)

Another example of dedication to art is offered by Vincent van Gogh. In one of his many letters to his brother Théo, he writes:

Painting is a form of love and to love is to give desperately of one's self.

These two ways of approaching art, van Gogh's and Mondrian's, are not mutually exclusive, rather they are personal views of the same thing. They share the common denominator of dedication, continuity, and an absolute love of art.

Now, let us return to the composition for the next step: cross-hatching.

After you have practiced outlining the shapes and defining the shadows with a soft charcoal pencil (no. 3) or charcoal chalk, spray your drawing lightly with fixative. Be sure to spray at least 20 inches from the surface. Otherwise, you risk spraying too much fixative in one area, causing irreparable damage. Not only does it leave spots on the drawing, but it is difficult to draw in any area with too much fixative on it.

Let your drawing dry for a few minutes, then, with a wide, flat brush (about 4 inches wide) or a soft cloth, lightly dust it, so you leave only a faint line behind.

Now, with a light hand and a well-sharpened piece of charcoal held at a 30-

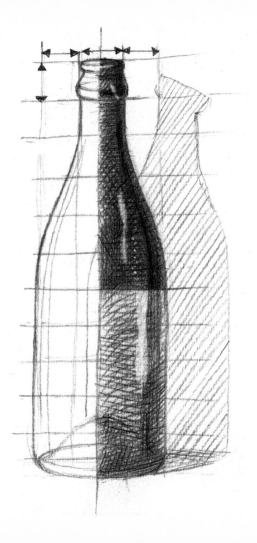

degree angle to the paper, hatch in the shadows you have drawn. Lightly spray on more fixative and dust. Next, go on to the darker areas of the objects, as well as the shadows you have already started, hatching them, at an angle, as before, but this time, work in the opposite direction, across the first hatching. You will have three tones of black and white: the white surface, a slightly defined dark area, and the darker shadows. Again, spray on fixative and dust.

Move on to the halftones, patiently hatching them in with vertical lines in an orderly fashion. Cover the entire drawing except for the areas in full light, going over the halftones, the dark parts of the objects, and the shadows.

If you stop and look at your drawing, you will notice that the picture is beginning to emerge like a black-and-white polaroid photograph developes. Spray on the fixative again and dust. Now go on hatching horizontally, this time going only over the darkest areas, then spray and dust again.

Repeat the hatching, at a 45-degree angle, in the darkest areas and the shadows; spray, and then go over the dark areas of the objects, hatching in the opposite direction. Spray and dust again.

Shade in the darkest areas; then, using a brush, cover the light areas with a thin layer of powdered charcoal.

Be careful to keep an eye on the gray tones. You should work on the darkest areas in stages. It is easy enough to make an object darker; it is not so easy to go back and make it lighter.

The last step is to emphasize the areas that receive the most light, using soft, white pastels or chalk, taking care not to overdo it.

You can achieve certain luminous effects by taking a clean kneadable putty eraser and gently rubbing the areas you want to highlight.

To keep the eraser clean, rub it frequently on a piece of stretched linen cloth or fine sandpaper.

Never use bread as an eraser as it is too greasy and it might smear the colors. An artist should understand all the uses of a tool like an eraser. As we have previously seen, it not only erases mistakes but can be used to highlight or remove traces of color as well.

Proper use of an eraser is important to the overall effect of a drawing as you can see if you study the different stages of the composition in the following pages.

Let us go on working with the geometric shapes used in the composition. You can practice by drawing several versions of each individual form on a single sheet. When you draw them, try to portray them from different angles.

Shape their outlines and, to avoid errors, observe the perspective carefully—it is quite easy to get the perspective or the angles wrong.

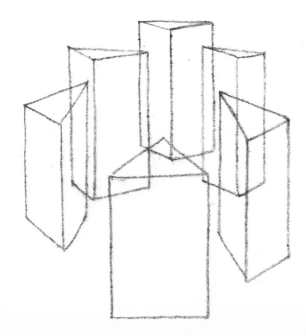

Now, let us do a composition in charcoal or sanguine using just the outlines. Keep in mind that modern artists have placed a great deal of importance on line.

In fact, even though this might seem to you like a beginners' exercise, it is not particularly easy and is actually a study for professionals.

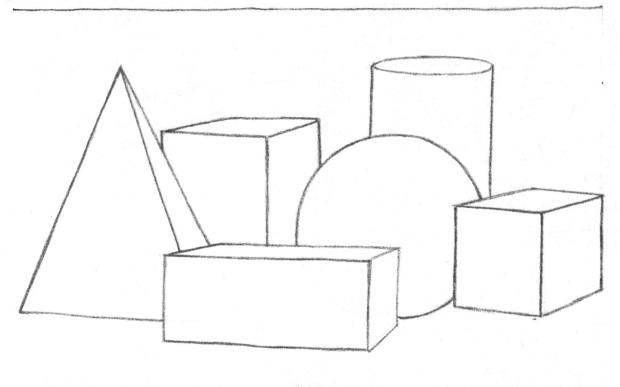

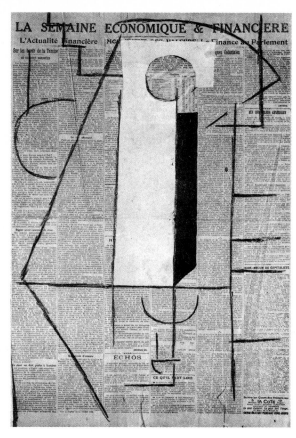

Pablo Picasso (1881-1973): Table with Bottle. *Mixed media with charcoal (24 ³/₈ × 17 ³/₈ in.). Picasso Museum, Paris.*

Of all the modern artists, Pablo Picasso, whose drawing is reproduced here, experimented the most with different techniques. He did innumerable still lifes, using just the strong lines of contour, and his cubist phase began after a very successful period as a figurative artist.

Picasso's first teacher was his father, José Ruiz Blasco, a good painter, who taught drawing at an art school. As a teacher, Ruiz was very disciplined and exacting; he probably demanded more of his son than of his other students. Picasso refused to use his father's name later, instead taking that of his mother. I suspect the desire to be better than his father pushed Picasso to become the great artist we know.

Look at this work on the left, which uses different media. It is a very uncomplicated cubist work, but notice the artist's use of charcoal. See how simple it is, yet full of emotion, and how precise and rhythmic the lines are.

Go back now and draw an outline of your composition. It can be made with either charcoal or sanguine. You should pay special attention to perspective and proportions. Brush your drawing with a soft cloth. If you are using sanguine, this will create the characteristic red haze that you can see in the background of my work. Go back over the lines again, this time tracing over them with one continuous line.

Using the same technique, try drawing a plant. Choose one you have at home and proceed as you did in the previous exercise.

A Plant in Charcoal and Sanguine

Now, try drawing a euphorbia plant, like the one on page 39, using both charcoal and sanguine. The euphorbia is an excellent subject because of the simplicity of its flowers and leaves as well as its structure. It almost looks as if nature had created it the way a child molds clay.

Begin by drawing an outline, using a hard charcoal pencil (no. 1) on a piece of semi-rough, off-white paper like cover stock.

Continue by shading the different tones of the leaves with very fine hatching in one direction. Half close your eyes and pick out the various shades of gray among the leaves. Make the leaves in the shadows darker than the others. Try to arrive at the darkest shades gradually, balancing and relating them to the lighter tones around them. This will give your drawing a proper sense of depth.

Do not forget that the red flowers should also be lightly shaded with the charcoal in all those parts which are in the shadow.

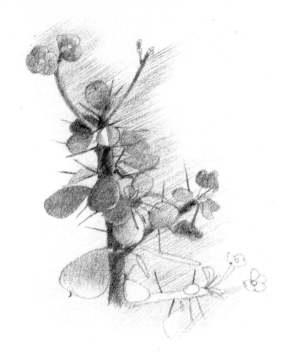

Spray a thin and even layer of fixative on your drawing and then, using a light touch, continue to color it with sanguine. When you are finished, go over it again with the fixative.

Drawing with Pastels

After you have practiced with charcoal and sanguine pencils, try your hand with colored pastels for a more chromatic effect.

The box of colored pastels is your palette; remember to keep the pastels in order and arranged according to color. On pages 44 and 45, you will find a chromatic scale showing the minimum number of colors you should have available.

The technique that should be the inspiration for your work with pastels is Pointillism. It consists of dabbing small dots of pure color over an extensive surface; the dots blend together giving the illusion of a single impression or color. Pointillism was an artistic technique developed in France at the end of the 19th century; in Italy it was known under the name of *Divisionismo* and two of its greatest representatives were Giovanni Segantini and Pellizza da Volpedo, whom we will discuss later in the book. The procedure adopted by the Pointillist painters reproduced light by methodically placing minute dots of complementary colors close together.

In order to emphasize an area of warm colors (reds or yellows), the artist would prepare a thin base of a cool color or, better yet, choose a paper or canvas in that color. To

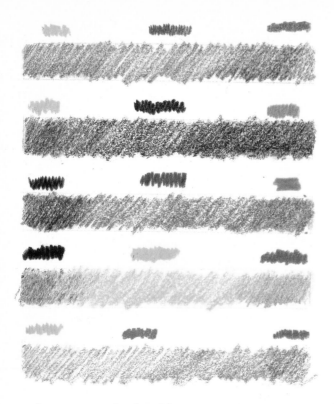

mind that when placed near its complement, a color becomes even darker and deeper. To bring a color out while keeping it a warm tone, add a little cadmium yellow.

The use of charcoal or sanguine can be decisive in working with pastels, so you must learn how to use both of them correctly and efficiently.

Now you are ready to try a pastel drawing yourself. The first step is always to sketch the composition, in a few lines, with a charcoal pencil. In a freehand sketch, it is the impression that one achieves that is most important. You should always work to convey your ideas with as few lines as possible.

Look at the sketches reproduced on the right. Note how little there is to distinguish the sketches by a modern artist from one by a Renaissance artist, yet in the final execution, these sketches became vastly different pictures.

But let us go back to your pastel drawing. Do all your work at one sitting, constantly referring to your subject. Learn to memorize its shape. The more you work from real life, the more sure of yourself you will become. Do not give up, even if you get tired. Keep practicing over and over again as if each drawing were the first.

play up a cool color (blue or green), he would use a warm color as a base.

Remember, if a color is too cool, it can be warmed up. For example, green can be warmed with a red or yellow. Also keep in

Paul Cézanne (1839-1906): above, Five Figures. *Charcoal (6×7¹/₄ in.); below,* The Boat Race. *Charcoal (⁴/₄×6⁵/₈ in.). Kunstmuseum Basel, Kupferstichkabinett.*

Tintoretto (1518-94): A Study for the Battle of Zara. *Charcoal (14×10⁵/₈ in.). Uffizi Gallery, Florence.*

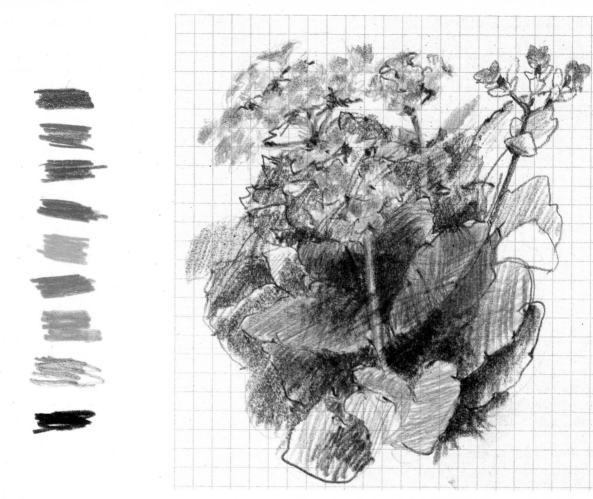

Just like charcoal drawings, pastels also must be done with confidence. Do not worry about mistakes; you can draw over them without bothering to erase. It is better to see two confident lines rather than a single one that is not.

To make this first exercise easier, at the left of the pastel, I have reproduced the colors I used.

Look for a kalanchoe plant in flower—it should be easy to find one in any plant nursery. Position the plant so that the light falls on it from the front. On whatever kind of paper you like, begin drawing a strong, black outline of the plant, shading in the shadows with charcoal. Without dusting, spray a light layer of fixative over it. After it is dry (this should take a few minutes), lay on the cool colors of the darkest leaves by using a malachite green pastel crayon. Color the leaves in the background by hatching them with long, light strokes of the same malachite green.

Next, using olive green, fill in the stems of the flower and the parts of the leaves in half-tones, and hatch the areas in full light with grass green. The reflections of light are achieved with a dark yellow.

Last, color the flowers by spreading dabs of dark vermilion red over them and by using orange in the lower areas that receive more light. Spray your work lightly with fixative, and go over the darkest areas with charcoal. Spray it again and your pastel is finished.

A Bowl of Eggs

Each project must begin with a good drawing, otherwise the final result will be jeopardized. A pastelist should never be satisfied with his first drawing. He must be very rigorous, because the number of colors at his disposal, no matter how many crayons he has, will never offer the range of chromatic possibilities that other media can. A chromatic effect similar to that of other media will only be achieved if you know how to lay down, superimpose, and shade colors, and in the process, learn to think.

Remember, just as continuity and building in stages are important to watercolors and tempera painting, a good foundation and technique are crucial to pastels.

If you look carefully at the preliminary sketches made by great artists, you will see their basic construction lines. The greater the artist, the more solid his basic construction work.

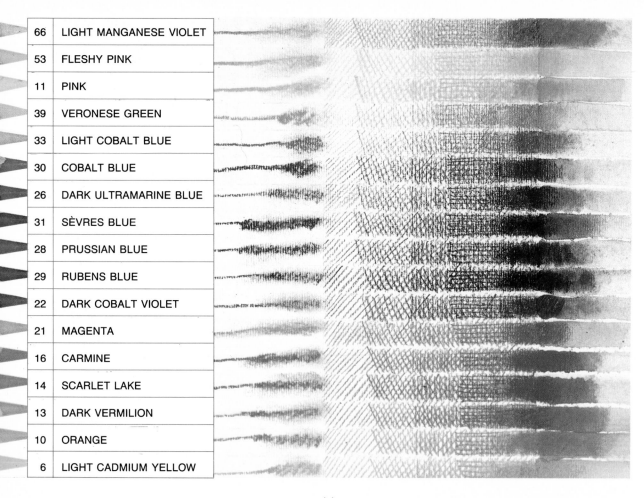

66	LIGHT MANGANESE VIOLET
53	FLESHY PINK
11	PINK
39	VERONESE GREEN
33	LIGHT COBALT BLUE
30	COBALT BLUE
26	DARK ULTRAMARINE BLUE
31	SÈVRES BLUE
28	PRUSSIAN BLUE
29	RUBENS BLUE
22	DARK COBALT VIOLET
21	MAGENTA
16	CARMINE
14	SCARLET LAKE
13	DARK VERMILION
10	ORANGE
6	LIGHT CADMIUM YELLOW

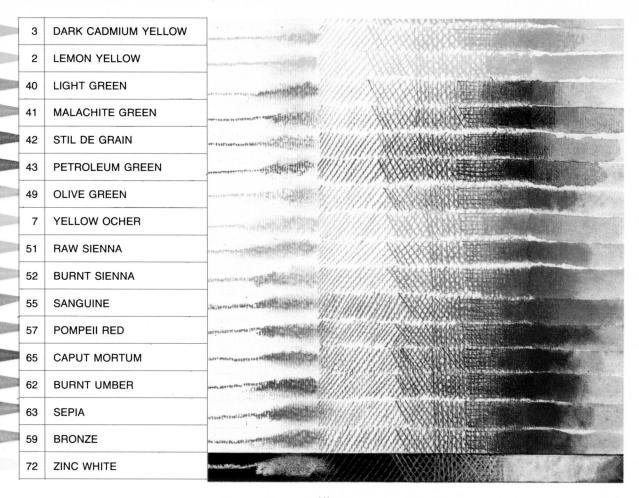

3	DARK CADMIUM YELLOW
2	LEMON YELLOW
40	LIGHT GREEN
41	MALACHITE GREEN
42	STIL DE GRAIN
43	PETROLEUM GREEN
49	OLIVE GREEN
7	YELLOW OCHER
51	RAW SIENNA
52	BURNT SIENNA
55	SANGUINE
57	POMPEII RED
65	CAPUT MORTUM
62	BURNT UMBER
63	SEPIA
59	BRONZE
72	ZINC WHITE

Corot, one of the precursors of the Impressionists, said:

The first two things to study are form and value. These two things are, I believe, the true foundations of art. Color and execution only add to the attractiveness of the work.

Learning to understand form is crucial.

Look at the next exercise I have prepared for you. It consists of a bowl of eggs. As you can see, the bowl is an oval, resting on an oval pedestal. And, because light is coming from above, it casts an oval shadow. The bowl is filled with eggs that are, of course, oval.

The construction of the ovals which constitute these figures and shadows follows the rules of perspective. These are too complex to be fully discussed here, so I will explain the practical points you will need to understand to begin work immediately. At the same

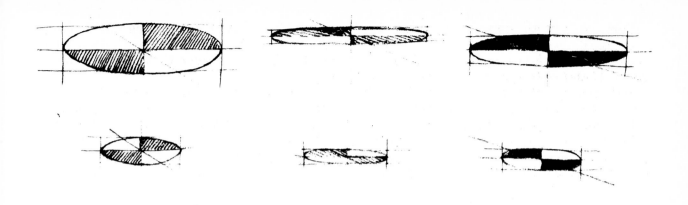

time, though, I want to teach you to look at things so you can resolve problems of perspective and construction by yourself.

First, sketch the bowl and eggs as if they were transparent. Draw the parts that are hidden as well as the parts you can see. If you do not use this little trick, the eggs will never look as though they were correctly placed inside the bowl. The process of drawing the complete object, including the parts normally not visible, has always been used by artists to give an impression of solidity.

For everything you draw, try to figure out the regular or irregular geometric shape it contains. In the case of the bowl, the oval fits within a rectangle. The higher you place your point of view, the wider the rectangle becomes. On the other hand, if you lower the point of view, the rectangle becomes narrower. Follow the same procedure for the base of the bowl.

Since the distance between the two ovals is minimal (so small that the rule for the vanishing point does not apply), you can sketch them using parallel lines. Make sure the lines representing the ovals are parallel. A mistake will make the object look as though it didn't rest on a flat base. Another

47

rule I suggest you follow is to divide the ovals into four parts. You will see that the four sections are symmetrically opposed, two by two. Try this out with different objects until it becomes automatic.

Returning to our sketch, another large oval forms the body of the bowl. This part, like getting the lines parallel, is somewhat

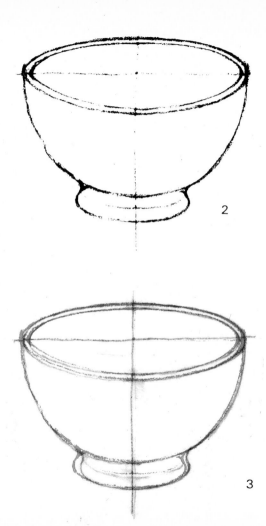

2

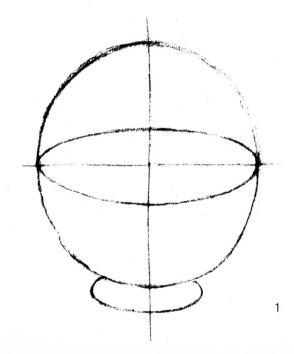

1

3

48

difficult. Move the charcoal over the paper continuously and evenly with a circular motion until, by using the two axes of the first oval, you begin to draw a second one, tangential to it (fig. 1 on p. 48). Erase the top half, and you will have made a well-constructed bowl that is harmonious as well as pleasing to look at (fig. 2 on p. 48).

Now by rounding off the edges, you can finish the bowl. But you are not done yet. Check if it has been drawn correctly by holding your picture at an angle in front of a mirror. The bottom of the paper should rest against the mirror. The reflection will reveal any of the mistakes your eye did not catch (fig. 3 on p. 48). Now, you need only make your final corrections.

A Pot of Geraniums Using Pastel Chalks

Pastels, especially when used on a rough surface, permit a great range of chromatic effects. With pastel chalks, you can work in broad areas as if you were painting with a wide, flat brush.

Look at the study of flowers I have reproduced on the following page and note the different phases of development.

The pastel was drawn on the rough side of a piece of cardboard lining taken from a fruit crate.

The surface does not need any special preparation. You only need to choose your subject and begin work. I advise you not to bother with details; just look at your subject as if it were a series of colored shapes. Pick a subject that you can draw as a broad mass. I would say a composition of geraniums is ideal, because of the shape of their leaves as well as the contrast of colors between them and the flowers.

Begin your drawing by sketching the subject with sanguine chalk, which is perfect for drawing very light, brownish-colored lines. For the background, where there are more objects visible, like the bucket, use a pastel chalk that is the same color as the object, and then continue with the other parts of the background.

Using a dark green, fill in all the leaves, one by one. Color the branches a natural, raw umber in the cooler areas and burnt umber in the warmer areas. For the areas in direct light, use raw sienna.

To color the background, make use of several shades of blue: an ultramarine blue for the halftones, indigo blue for the darkest

areas, and electric blue for the lightest ones.

When you are finished with the background, highlight the leaves with a bright green chalk.

Now color the flowers. Use a red lacquer or carmine red for the base color and go over the lightest parts of the petals with vermilion red or yellow-orange.

The Conservatory, a Pastel by Emilio Gola

Emilio Gola, descendant of one of the most aristocratic families in Lombardy, was born in Milan in 1852. He chose art as his vocation and began his career very early, sketching the Milanese literary and intellectual avant-garde. At the beginning, his work was hard to distinguish from the other artists of his time like Conconi, Gignous, Bianchi, and others. It was only later, after 1890, as he came into contact with Impressionism and absorbed its techniques, that Gola developed a more personal style.

Emilio Gola was a kind of prophet to the Lombardy youth of his time. Misunderstood by the critics, he was considered a controversial figure because he searched for spirituality in art and frankly renounced the kind of compromises which business often forced. He felt, when business and art mixed, that art always lost out. Gola died in 1925 with the worry that he had not finished his work. He often said:

I have so few years left, every minute that passes I must draw.

Known principally as a painter of the Navigli—the old canals that once ran through Milan, but which have now for the most part disappeared, covered over by roads—Gola also did a number of pastels using other subjects. The pastel reproduced on the following page, *The Conservatory*, painted in 1920, has an incredible freshness to it, with rich, bold colors reminiscent of the Impressionists. The picture is executed in pastel chalks on cardboard ($30 \times 20^{1/2}$ inches). The colors are put down thickly with a broad-based palette and few details; the greens contrast with the blues, yellows, ochers, etc.

Before we go on to the next chapter on figure and portrait drawing, I urge you to practice time and again the exercises we have discussed here. Try to figure out the colors in your subject and imitate them. Above all, never be satisfied with your first attempt. Practice over and over, always trying to improve.

Emilio Gola (1852-1925): The
Conservatory *(c. 1920). Pastel (30×20$^{1}/_{2}$ in.).*
Private Collection.

THE FIGURE AND THE PORTRAIT

The figure has always been a subject of great interest to artists, and through the centuries they have transformed and even revolutionized our way of seeing, interpreting, and drawing it.

Until figure drawing became part of the basic curriculum of art schools, anatomy lessons were given by university teachers using real cadavers. Over time, however, this method of teaching was abandoned. Today in art schools, the study of anatomy, even using plaster casts, is rarely taught. The result is that the ability to draw a good figure has almost been lost, and by "good," I mean one that is harmonious and delicate. If it is standing, it seems to be firmly planted on the ground; if it is sitting or lying down, it seems languid and relaxed.

In his *Treatise on Painting*, Leonardo da Vinci comments on the need for the artist to be familiar with human anatomy:

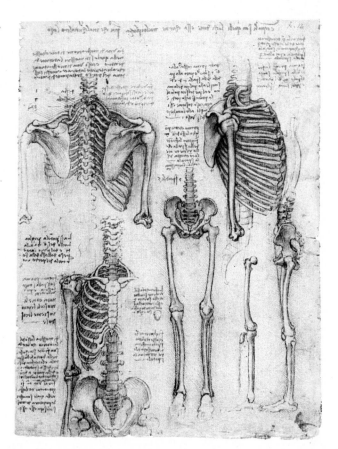

Leonardo da Vinci (1452-1519): Skeleton of the Torso and Legs. *Mixed media (11¹/₄ × 7⁷/₈ in.). Royal Library, Windsor.*

53

It is necessary for the painter, if he is to be a good portrayer of the attitudes and gestures of the nude figure, to know the anatomy of the nerves, bones, and muscles, so that he will know, for the different movements and tensions, what nerves or muscles are responsible for them, and emphasize those alone and not the others, as do many artists who, wanting to seem great draftsmen, make their nudes look stiff and graceless, more like bags of walnuts than human flesh, bunches of radishes instead of muscular nudes.

The more analytical an artist can be about human anatomy, the better he will construct a figure. It will also make him more inventive and help him penetrate the soul of his subjects. All this, however, demands an unconditional dedication to art.

To say these things in the age of computers may seem to be swimming against the current, but I do not see it this way. Instead, I predict a return eventually to large figurative art. I have always felt it better to finish only a few good works a year rather than many mediocre ones; not confusing quality with quantity (as commercial logic would have you do).

In the 14th century Cennino Cennini wrote in his *Book of Art* or *Treatise on Painting*:

What to Do if You Are Interested in Art

You, who with gentle spirit so love art, first put on these garments: love, awe, obedience and perserverance. And as soon as you can, place yourself in the hands of a good master and stay with him as long as you can.

In this guide, I will show you some anatomy studies by the great masters and, where possible, the rules they followed. I have selected the ones I think are the most important—though some of the studies use material other than charcoal or sanguine.

The three views in the illustration on the opposite page may be of help in understanding how the human skeleton is drawn. The drawing on the right is an unfinished sketch made following the rules of proportions. The middle drawing, front view, leaves only the arms unfinished. The one on the left shows a side view of the skeleton fully drawn and shaded.

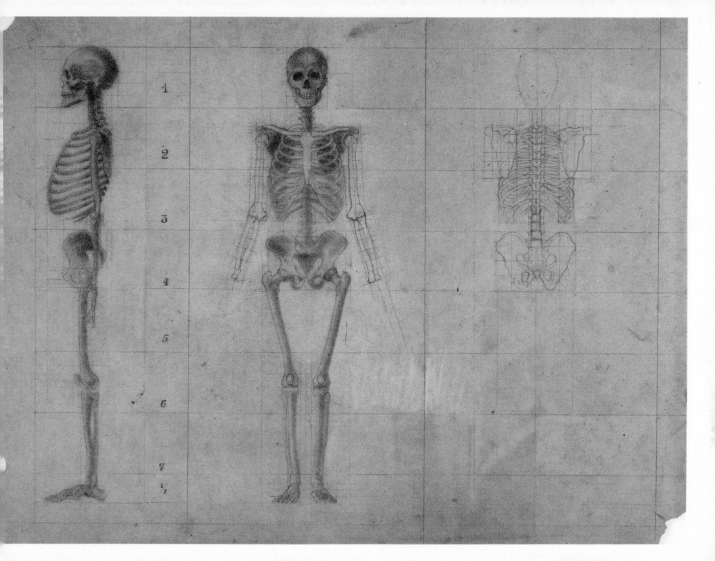

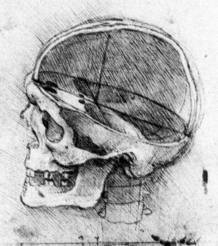

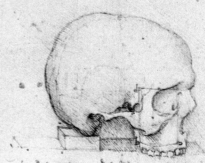

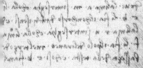

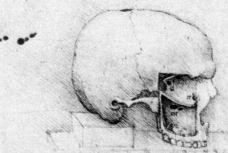

The Unity of Measurement

The basic unit used to construct the human figure is the head. The length of the body, from head to toe, should be seven and one half times the length of the head.

Since it is not easy to get hold of a human skeleton, I would suggest you begin by going to your local science museum and copying one from its collection. First, use sheets of grid paper. Afterward you can go back to cover stock or brown wrapping paper and draw the skeleton on a larger scale.

Start by copying the skeleton in profile, beginning with the head, and continue to construct the drawing of your skeleton carefully using the proportions of seven and a half times the head measurement (see the sketches on page 55).

You can look at reproductions of old masters' drawings for details of the anatomy if you need help. (Leonardo da Vinci is especially good, as he was the first to reproduce the skeleton, muscles, and organs of the human body.) Next, draw the skeleton from the front and back, following the rules of projection.

It is very important to be able to draw the skull well. Try to sketch it from all angles—from the front, in profile, and in a three-quarters profile taken from both the left and from the right.

The study of Leonardo da Vinci, reproduced here, with its sequence of heads, is a useful example of this exercise. Practice by copying these drawings. Using a sharp sanguine pencil, enlarge the head and fill in the shadows and highlights. (If you are interested in pursuing this further, you can look for plaster casts of skulls in art supply stores.)

Turn now to my study of the skull on page 58, in which I have made the construction lines clearly visible. Try to copy the plaster cast, using the same methods of construction I used.

Always draw meticulously, sketching what you see, not what you think. Before you even draw the first line, look at your subject again. Do not trust your eyes alone. Use a plumb line and pencil to verify the perpendicular lines, if necessary.

Look at the study of a head by Cézanne on

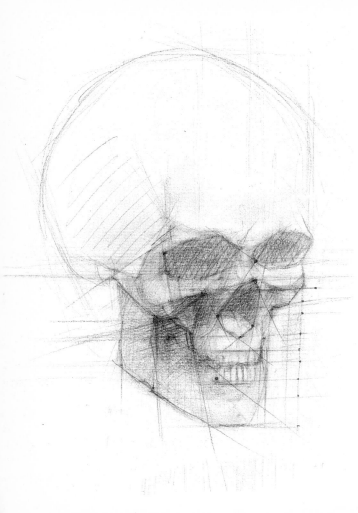

page 59. You will notice that he uses a great many lines, one right next to the other. This creates an almost palpable feeling of vibration and was the secret of this great artist. Since he had little academic training, he was very critical of his own work. This proved to be an impetus that pushed him to look for and create a new style of art. I have copied an extract from a letter Rainer Maria Rilke wrote to his wife about Cézanne, which sheds more light on his character.

Rue Cassette 29, Paris VI, 9 October 1907

Today I want to describe Cézanne for you. As for his work, he said that he had lived a bohemian life until he was forty. It was only after he met Pissarro that he had any desire to work. But then it was in such measure that for the next thirty years, work is all he did. He seemed to do it joylessly, in a sustained fury, and he was always dissatisfied with what he had done. He never seemed to achieve what he considered to be the essential. He called this "accomplishment" and he found it in the Venetians, whose works he first saw in the Louvre and later over and over again; he recognized their accomplishment without reserve. The test, "making some-

Paul Cézanne: Study of the
Skull *(c. 1900). Pencil
(7⅝×4¾ in.). Kunstmuseum
Basel, Kupferstichkabinett.*

thing," a reality reached thanks to his experience of an object and its indestructibility, was what he considered his true work to be. Old, sick, reduced each evening to exhaustion from his daily work (to the point that after distractedly eating his supper, he would go to bed at six), malicious, distrustful, derisive every time he went to his studio, sneering, badly treated—yet he observed Sunday, going to Mass and vespers like a child and politely asking Madame Brémond, the landlady, for a better meal—perhaps he hoped each day to achieve the results he considered so essential. And so he burdened his work in the most stubborn way (if one can believe a reporter of the day he was not a very likeable painter who pandered to everyone). To sketch a landscape or still life, he planted himself firmly before his subject and would begin only after very complicated convolutions.

He would begin with very dark colors and then he would cover over them with tones just slightly lighter, shading one color with another until he had created a figure, and then he would move on to the next one, contrasting the first with the second and so on. I think the two things, the actual object he saw and its reality, and his appropriation, his personal use of it, were at odds and fought within him, perhaps following a prick of conscience, and they would begin, as it were, to speak to him at the same time, constantly interrupting each other, splitting him in two, nonstop.

And the old man would put up with this discord and move on...

(*Lettere su Cézanne*, Electa, Milan, 1984)

What I said before about studying the bone structure holds true not only for the head but for the other parts of the body as well. It is important to understand how the body moves. You must have seen drawings where the body looked awkward or was in an impossible position. This comes from not thoroughly knowing the bone structure of the body.

I think it is worthwhile to look at some more of Leonardo da Vinci's studies of anatomy. The images that follow speak for themselves. It is up to you to study them and copy them with an analytical eye.

Facing page, left to right: Leonardo da Vinci: Arm Movements controlled by the Biceps. *Mixed Media (8⁵/₈ × 7⁷/₈ in.).* Bones of the Foot and Shoulder. *Mixed Media (11¹/₄ × 7⁷/₈ in.). Royal Library, Windsor. Following page: Leonardo da Vinci*: Leg Bones. *Mixed Media (11¹/₄ × 7⁷/₈ inc.). Royal Library, Windsor.*

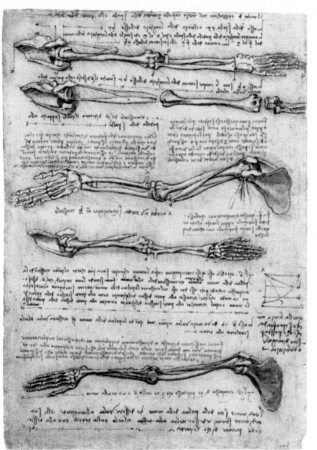

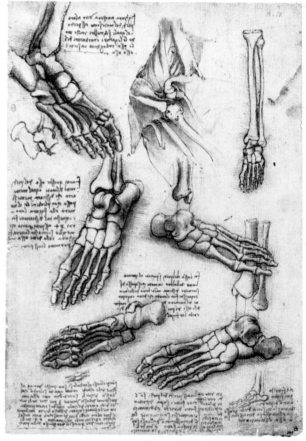

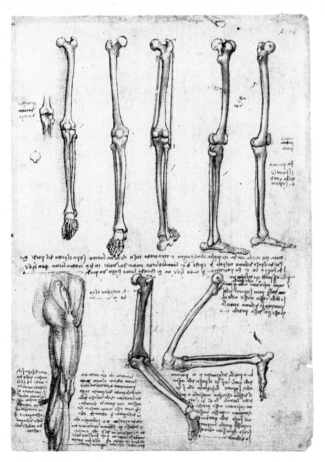

The Muscle Structure

Once you have studied the bone structure and practiced drawing it, you can move on to the study of muscles. Remember, continuity and a good technique are the bases of a good artist.

Giuseppe Pellizza da Volpedo

A few years ago I went to a large exhibition of the works of Giuseppe Pellizza da Volpedo in Alexandria. I went without much enthusiasm because I had always considered him to be a rather minor provincial artist, at least, that was how he had been presented to me at school. The exhibition was an eye-opener and forced me to reconsider completely my way of thinking about this great artist.

Born in 1868, he studied in Brera from 1883 to 1887, attending classes in modeling and etching. In 1888 he transferred to the Accademia di Belle Arti in Florence, where Giovanni Fattori taught.

He went to Paris in 1889 and returned in 1890 to participate in exhibitions throughout Italy. When Giovanni Segantini died in 1899, the Pointillists turned to Pellizza da Volpedo hoping to find in him Segantini's heir. Yet even in 1900, he was still not able

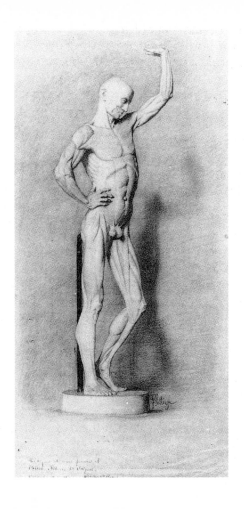

to make an independent living as a painter and frequently had to ask his parents for financial help.

He spent ten years of exhausting effort on his most famous work, *The Fourth State*, which he exhibited at the Quadriennale Torinese, in 1901, hoping to win a prize. But with its clear social statement, the painting won nothing; in fact, it was not even sold. Not until 1907, in Rome, was he able to show the picture without creating a scandal. But by then the artist, burdened by family problems and exhausted by work, had lost all hope. At the age of 39, Pellizza da Volpedo took his own life.

Gino Severini, the Futurist painter, wrote:

I met Pellizza da Volpedo once in Rome and I liked him very much, both as a painter and as a person. In fact, I must say that the way he thought out and composed his paintings, like a primitive, and the love he put into his works pleased and charmed me, because I saw something of myself in it.

With the rise of fascism, Pellizza da Volpedo was forgotten. People are only now

Pellizza da Volpedo (1868-1907): Anatomy Showing Muscles. *Charcoal (25⅝ × 12¼ in.). Private Collection, Turin.*

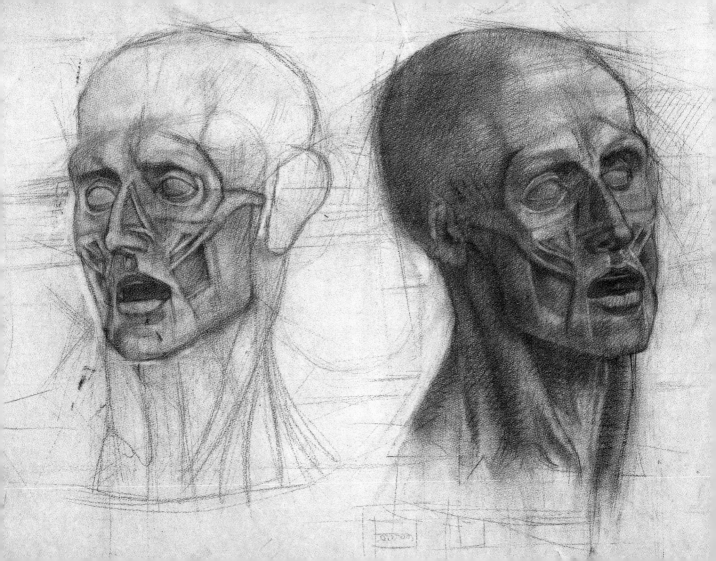

discovering that he was not as provincial as some second-rate art critics would have led us to believe.

His anatomical drawings from his academic period reveal just how accomplished he was and what a mistake it is to ignore him. He used charcoal with great skill and, in each of his studies, he maintained the importance of volume.

I have reproduced a study by Pellizza da Volpedo on page 63 to give him the attention I feel he deserves.

A Study of the Head Muscles

To learn anatomy correctly, it is best to start with the basic unit of measurement, the head. A medical textbook on anatomy would be another good place to start from. Knowing the muscles and how they function is very important.

Another good tool is a plaster cast of a head that shows anatomical detail, like those used in art schools. Practice drawing it from every possible angle. I do a series of studies like this once a year.

When you draw the head, note all the points where the horizontal and vertical lines meet. Make use of the plumb line and a pencil, as I described in the first chapter.

Do a series of drawings on a single sheet, as you did with the skeleton, referring back to the ones you have already done for the right proportions. Pretend you are doing the sketches for an animated cartoon, and make only minimal changes in each drawing in the series.

Place the head you plan to copy at eye level, with the light falling from one side so the shadows accentuate the muscles.

Always make your drawing smaller than actual size rather than larger. When you are more confident, you can do them full-size. This is very important; if you do larger-than-life drawings, your eyes cannot take in everything at once.

Anatomy by Giorgio Balconi

Giorgio Balconi and I both attended art school in the Castello Sforzesco, which had excellent classical teachers. Luciano Gussoni, in our second year, and Virginio Bertazzoni, who taught fresco painting, were two demanding, disciplined, and passionate teachers, who managed to instill in us some of these qualities.

Balconi and I with a few other students formed a tightly-knit group. We never lacked determination or drive, even when we had spent the whole morning working at our jobs (which allowed us to continue our studies—we were from working-class families, and our parents had little money to invest in our futures as artists).

With the enthusiasm of sixteen-year-olds, we rented a studio in a walk-up apartment building in the old section of Milan. We spent long hours there, experimenting, discussing, and arguing about our ideas and our work.

Then, as it so often happens, after a few years the group split up, and we went our separate ways. Some gave up their chalks and brushes for good, others continued. A few took roads that were still somehow linked to art. Giorgio Balconi, still a good friend today, is now a graphic artist working in advertising. Recently I came across some of his anatomy studies, which are only a part of the work he did in his school days. They were so good that I decided to reproduce his instead of some of my own.

Anatomy should be studied beginning with the head, then moving on to the torso, legs, and arms. As an exercise, find a statue of a full figure to copy. Sketch the head lightly on a large surface, leaving some space around it. Then go back over it,

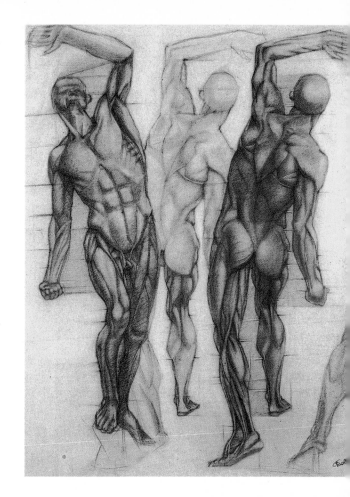

modifying and correcting it until you have given it more detail. Now do the same with the torso, legs, arms, hands, and feet, going back over, adding more detail each time.

When you are satisfied with these sketches, draw them from another angle, with new reference points, following the same steps.

If you look at Balconi's anatomies, you will see the parts that look the most finished are also the most correctly constructed, while the less finished parts are still out of proportion. Constructing an anatomy is a slow, precise process. Here logic and knowledge should be linked to what we see and draw.

Studying anatomy may seem boring to you, but it should not be. It is only boring if badly taught or done by someone who does not like to draw. But if it is studied properly, in theory and in practice, the drawing of a human figure can produce the same emotion as drawing an Impressionist landscape.

Because no one talks about art and anatomy with much enthusiasm these days, the way I look at it may seem rather outdated to you. But if you do not know anything about anatomy, how can you draw a portrait so it has the right expression?

The lines of construction in anatomy are marvelous architecture. Piet Mondrian was so inspired by these lines, that he based some of his abstract paintings on them.

Anatomy of the Hand by Pellizza da Volpedo

Turn to page 68 and look at how the artist was able to make a white plaster cast come alive. Pellizza da Volpedo drew this hand when he was only sixteen.

A good education is very important, of course, but you also need a passionate desire to learn. As Leonardo da Vinci said:

... great love is born from deep knowledge of the thing you love. If you do not know it well, you will not truly be able to love it. If you love it for what you hope to get from it and not for its intrinsic value, you are like the dog jumping up and down and wagging its tail at its master, hoping for a bone from him. If that same dog understood his master's virtues, he would love him much more, for he would love him for himself.

I urge young artists to look for good teachers—and this does not necessarily mean the most famous, for fame is not al-

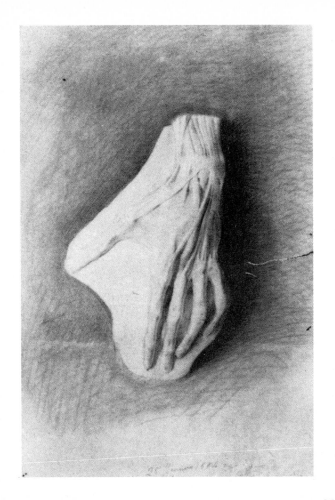

ways a true indication of ability. A hundred years ago, a formal academic education was the foundation of all artists' training, and I still think it is a good way to start.

Anatomical Drawings by Michelangelo and Leonardo da Vinci

The drawing by Michelangelo, reproduced on the right, was a preliminary study for a figure, the Lybian Sibyl, in the frescoes of the Sistine Chapel at the Vatican.

Notice how the hatching, done in sanguine, for the skin and the muscle suggested underneath it is not done only in one direction, but instead follows the contours of the body and darkens in the areas of heaviest shadow. As you can see, the outline of the figure is thinnest where the light falls directly on it and is thickest where it is most in shadow.

Look at Leonardo da Vinci's study of the neck and shoulder on the following page and notice the wonderful attention to detail.

Left: Pellizza da Volpedo: Anatomy of the Hand. *Charcoal (18⁷/₈×13 in.). Maria Pellizza Collection, Volpedo. Right: Michelangelo Buonarroti (1475-1564)*: Page from Studies for the Lybian Sibyl. *Sanguine (11⁹/₈×8³/₈ in.). Metropolitan Museum of Art, New York.*

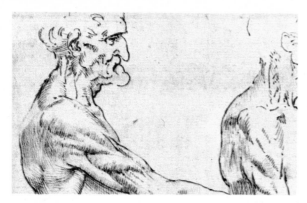

Leonardo da Vinci: Anatomical Representation of the Neck and Shoulder Muscles *(detail). Mixed Media (11¹/₄ × 7⁷/₈ in.). Royal Library, Windsor.*

Two Drawings by Pablo Picasso

Most people think of Picasso as a painter of rather incomprehensible pictures, but he was an outstanding figurative artist. We will look at two of his drawings on the following page to see how a large figure in charcoal is done.

Picasso made this drawing when he was eleven. It reminds me of the high school exercises on costructing a profile, which were so typical of teaching methods at the end of the 19th century. Sadly, such exercises are no longer practiced today.

The first sketch, on the left, has been done schematically. The alignment is: forehead to nose, nose to chin, and a line going through the center of the eye, perpendicular to a line at the edge of the mouth. A teacher probably showed Picasso how to construct it, using as a model a plaster bust or a drawing in a book.

The drawing next to it is more finished, and here, Picasso begins to reveal his talent as he repeats the first construction, adding details and depth.

I found a similar exercise in an old book on drawing from the beginning of this century and have reproduced it for you on the next pages.

As you will see, there is a similarity between Picasso's drawings and these. The latter were not made as exercises for a high school class, but for a typical fourth- or fifth-grade class, that is, for ten- or eleven-year-olds. Nevertheless, it is a useful exercise for anyone learning to draw.

It is interesting to see how the problems of eye expressions were resolved. Notice, for example, that the iris is always partially covered by the eyelid and the middle of the ear is more or less lined up with the middle of the eye.

Pablo Picasso: Studio of Left Profile of an Old Man *(1892-93). Charcoal (9³/₈×12¹/₄ in.). Heirs of the Artist.*

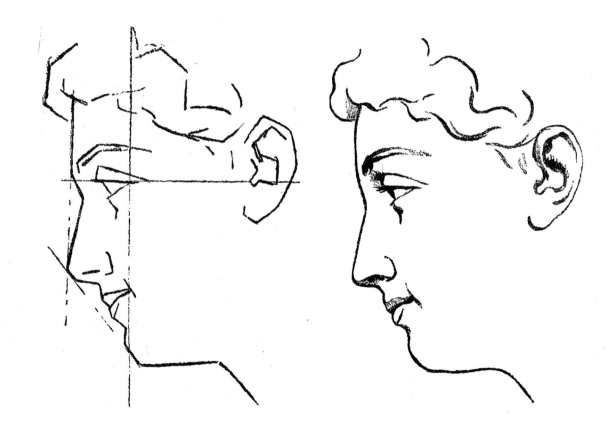

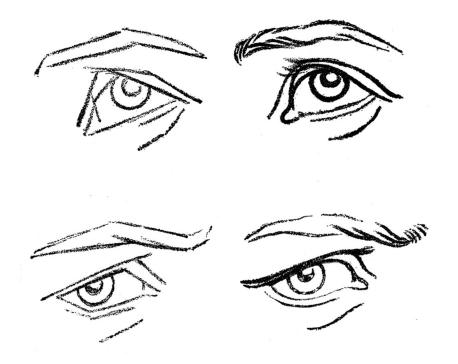

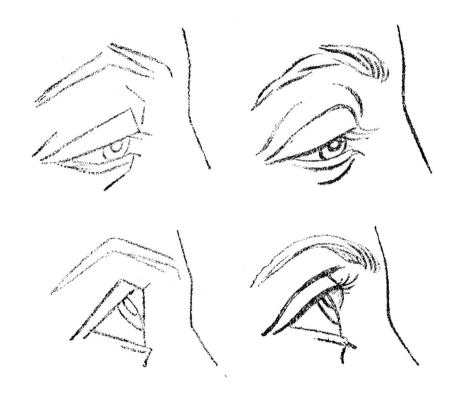

75

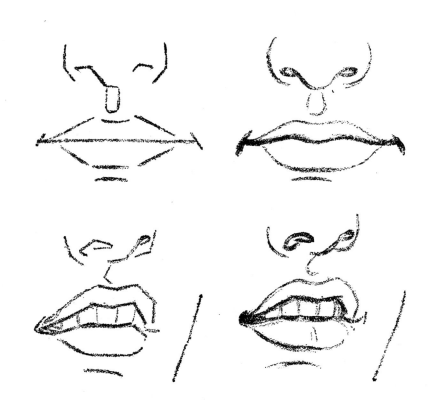

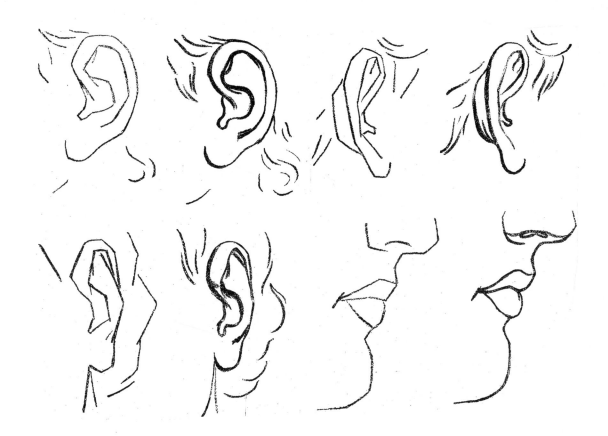

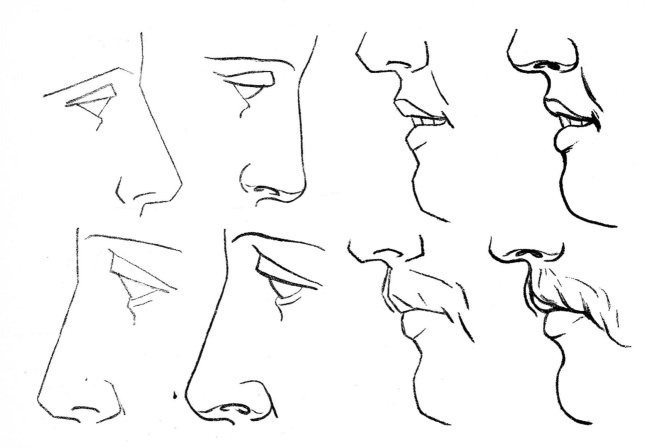

79

But the most impressive drawing is this one made by Picasso when he was only twelve. It is outlined with Conté crayons and shows the confidence of an expert—I did not do drawings such until I was twenty.

Drawing a Model from Life

There are a few rules to follow when you are drawing a live model.

Have your model assume a comfortable position, and before you let her take a break, mark in chalk the points of contact on the body (elbows, etc.) so she can return to the exact same position. Also, let her rest at least 5 minutes for every 20-25 minutes of posing.

First, have your model pose sitting, especially if she is not a professional.

Let us look now at our drawings. Look carefully at the construction of the seated figures on the right, seen both in profile and facing us, and try to analyze their construction. Then, see if you can find a model with the same physical characteristics and have her sit in the same position. Using the rougher side of a piece of white wrapping paper and some soft charcoal about $^3/_8$ inch

Pablo Picasso: Seated Man Covering His Face with His Hands *(1893). Charcoal (20³/₈ × 14³/₈ in.). Heirs of the artist.*

80

in diameter, lightly sketch an outline of your model. Spray it with a thin film of fixative, and then go back over the contours with a heavier line.

Next, have your model pose standing up and repeat your study in the same way you did the other.

I would suggest you choose a slender

model to begin with and gradually work up to one who has more flesh on her. Draw your first lines without erasing, then spray them, and go back over the contours. As you do several line studies, you will notice that if the construction is good, the drawing is much stronger.

Some Charcoal Figures by Edvard Munch, Pellizza da Volpedo, and Pablo Picasso

It is very important to learn how to "read" a picture, and the first thing to do is to find out how old the painter was when he made it. Compare, for example, some charcoals drawn by Pablo Picasso, Pellizza da Volpedo, and Edvard Munch when these artists were between fifteen and twenty-six. For an art student, these are formative years, when you begin the real adventure of art and the fires of passion are kindled. At this stage the student strives for perfection, laying down the foundation that will eventually develop into a personal style and direction.

I chose these three artists because, beside their obvious talents, they were all born in

Right and far right: Edvard Munch (1863-1944): Two Male Nudes, Standing (1899). *Charcoal (24³/₄ × 8³/₄ in.) and (28³/₈ × 19¹/₂ in.). Munch Museum, Oslo.*

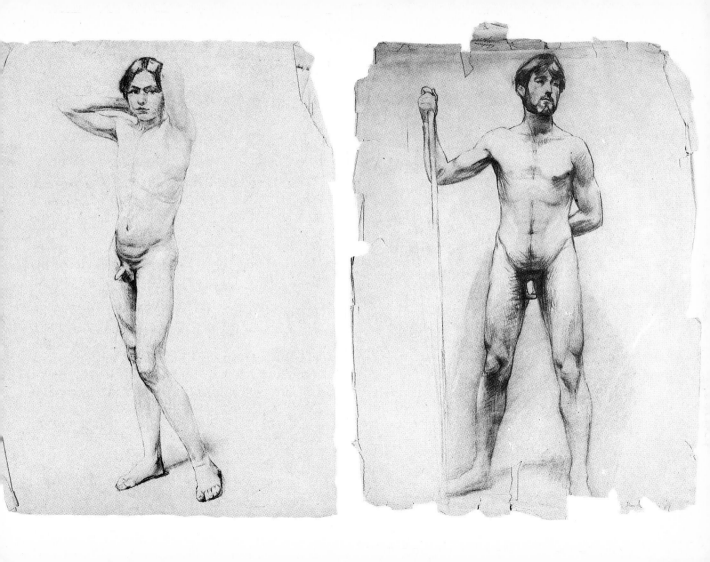

more or less the same period, that is, the second half of the 19th century (Munch in 1863, Pellizza in 1868, and Picasso in 1881), and they represent three different currents in art. Their common denominator is the wonderfully solid academic training they received from their respective art schools. Until about sixty years ago, these schools were like Renaissance workshops, and the excellence and discipline of the teachers made it possible for the students to express themselves fully.

In the two delicate charcoal sketches by Munch on page 83, so solid and carefully constructed, the artist lets us catch a glimpse of his very demanding early training. The shading is obtained with delicate cross-hatching; he uses neither a torchon nor a brush. The overall effect is a light patina of sadness.

Edvard Munch's paintings and graphics were instrumental in the development of Expressionism, conveying all the existential angst and anxiety connected with the social and psychological conditions of the time. His own personal tragedies occurred in 1868, when his mother died of tuberculosis (he was five), and in 1877 when he lost his beloved sister Sophie. These two events influenced all his work.

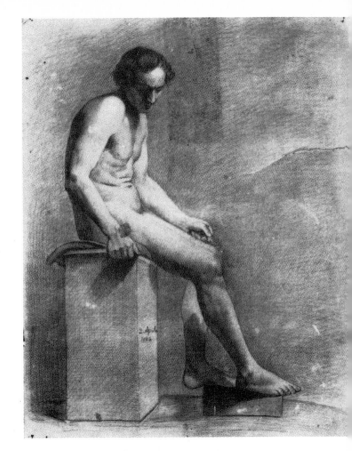

Pellizza da Volpedo: Seated Figure *(1884). Charcoal (23³/₄×18 in). Maria Pellizza Collection, Volpedo.*

Pellizza da Volpedo also had an excellent education. Through his work, he tried to show the exhausting life of the working man, the misery he suffered, and the strength and bravery that kept him going.

His nude reproduced here on the left, done with charcoal, is shaded with a broad brush, sprayed, and then filled in with delicate cross-hatching. The figure is like a column holding up a temple. Though it is in a resting position, it seems strong enough to bear up under any misfortune, fatigue, or pain.

Pablo Picasso drew the nude reproduced on the right when he was fifteen. He already liked to express himself violently and shockingly. He shaded the small areas with his finger and the larger ones with a cloth. The highlights were made by dusting the area with a brush until he had removed every trace of charcoal. Because he sprayed it with fixative at each different stage, at least three or four times while he worked, he obtained an almost three-dimensional quality. You can achieve a similar effect by using a combination of torchon, brush, and white pastel chalk to highlight your drawing.

Pablo Picasso: Seated Made Nude (1896). Charcoal ($23^5/_8 \times 18^1/_2$ in.). Picasso Museum, Barcelona.

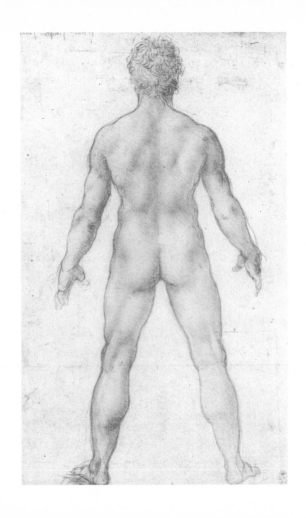

A Delicate Nude by Leonardo da Vinci

Let us go back once more to Leonardo da Vinci and look at a nude he did in sanguine. The model he chose is very robust and used to heavy physical labor. From the way his muscles are developed, he could have been a bricklayer or a blacksmith. To find someone with a similar physique today, you might look for a boxer.

Studying this nude, you can see how well Leonardo da Vinci knew human anatomy and the extraordinary ability he had for shading his figures. The light falls on his model from above and shows off the musculature of the body, while the shading follows the contours of the muscles. The hands are open like a fighter's, ready for anything that comes. The legs are positioned to give solidness to the figure. Leonardo da Vinci had such a sure knowledge of the human body, as well as the theory of shading, that he could draw a nude like this from his imagination or from the memory of someone he had seen.

Leonardo da Vinci: A Nude Seen from the Back. Sanguine ($10^5/_8 \times 6^1/_4$ in.). Royal Library, Windsor.

A Nude in Pastels by Gianni Maimeri

Gianni Maimeri is a completely unknown artist both to Italians and to the rest of the world.

Italy is a strange country. At every turn one is surprised by its beauty, its taste, its imagination. Yet, at the same time, it can be superficial, ignoring things right under its nose, and only seeing something when it is pointed out. This is the case with Gianni Maimeri. Not willing to compromise and meet the demands of the artistic establishment, he was ignored by those in the business of art (critics, art gallery owners, etc). But because I have read his notes and have seen his work, I want to bring more attention to him.

I asked for one of his pastels and I was given this drawing, reproduced on page 88, of his young wife lying in tender abandon.

Many artists have seen and portrayed their companions as symbols of sweetness and gentleness, the image of the woman that each would like by his side. This is in part, perhaps, compensation for the courage these women have shown in agreeing to share their lives with an artist. Busy with their work, artists can be capricious and unpredictable—stubborn one moment and vulnerable the next. We have an idea of Maimeri's feelings toward his wife from this figure done in pastels. He has captured the image of her as a young woman, immortalizing her soft, young beauty.

The work was done on cover stock, using pastel chalks which he shaded with his finger. The colors were first spread over the lighter areas of the drawing and then over the darker ones. He then blended the colors with his thumb, moving either from left to right or top to bottom.

In the areas that correspond to rounded parts of the body, he used a finger to shade them, with movements similar to a sculptor modeling clay.

In Maimeri's notes I found an incomplete draft of his theory of color with some definitions and interpretations of color terms. You should also try to create a personal "palette," that is, a chromatic range of ideas which reflects your personality and characterizes your work.

Begun December 10, 1932

I would like to attempt a study of color. To see its function after having established its character, that is, to try to define it.

Gianni Maimeri (1884-1951): Female Nude. *Pastels (39³/₈ × 78³/₄ in.). Private Collection.*

Different kinds of color

Physical color: *Specific vibrations of light*

Color as a material: *The colored substance a painter uses*

Ordinary color: *The tint of objects*

Painting color: *The variations of tint that an object undergoes in the physical world (and its relationship with the visual nature of the painter)*

Tone color: *The relationship between two colors in the same environment*

Pure color: *The colors in the spectrum in their truest state*

Physical tone or gradation: *The colors of the spectrum with black or white added, making them more or less luminous (when black is added) or more or less pure (when white is added)*

Chiaroscuro: *The shading from white to black of a highlighted object that is either deprived of color or is uniform in color*

Value: *The measure of the tonal diversity among different painting colors*

Intonation:

Harmony: *A constant relationship with reference to a basic color*

Tint: *A color taken by itself, removed from its environment (1944)*

Color tone: *The chiaroscuro relationship between two colors of different tints (1944)*

Complementary colors: *Colors to which the normal eye form a neutral color image with their composition*

Aura: *The exact repetition of a key color around its center of interest (1944)*

Integral harmony:

Influences:

Model colors:

Sensation colors:

Transformed color:

Pontillism:

Sensory Pointillism:

Nostalgic colors:

Meteorological colors:

Perfume colors:

Sound colors:

Invisible colors: *Colors which enter a composition as a result of an aura relationship.*

When we speak of color, very common concepts are expressed with wide latitude. Like all concepts of this kind, the expression remains uncertain, especially if the proposition touches on a subject which by nature is quite specific and limited, such as those that deal with problems of the spirit.

Wanting to discuss the function of color in painting seems vain and pointless since its relevance seems so obvious. Yet, if we keep to a limited area of common definitions, we can see how disparate these functions are, depending on who is looking at them. If you try to classify the physical phenomenon, its emotional function and the connection in a work of its correlative equivalence, the disparities multiply, depending on the schools, the basic tendencies of the artist, and his receptive possibilities.

List the definitions.

Therefore, mostly for my own use, and sticking to the meanings that most people understand, while at the same time using new concepts and expressions, I will establish a list of names that can make the concepts that develop clearer and more distinct.

Why this rearrangement of vocabulary is necessary.

The mistaken idea that in the hierarchy of phenomena, color holds a very low position.

The classical academic concept of the supremacy of form. Incomplete definition of the concept of drawing. The drawing is not the outline and is not the contours, and these two operations, alone or together, do not generate or esthetically express form.

The mistake of looking for hierarchies.

The error of the critic who places the value of the work of art on the form motive when it is really the color motive that influences him.

Even the most enlightened critics have always given a secondary role to color both in art and in life.

Color is not an unimportant superimposition or an adornment of reality, and thus of art, but one of the manifestations of the essence of a thing. It is only different in the way it is classified by physicists according to certain natural laws. It becomes inseparable from reality by the perception of the artist, through whom, in the act of seeing, it becomes reality, because the eye sees everything in color.

You should try to keep such notes. Write them in a notebook as they occur to you. It will help you create your own personal theory of art, as well as a greater understanding of the process.

Woman Bathing by Edgar Degas

The official art world in France exploded in 1874. That year a group of young artists organized their own exhibition in the photographer Nadar's studio. Their show was in opposition to the official exhibition at the Salon, which had so often refused their work.

Most of the works exhibited at Nadar's

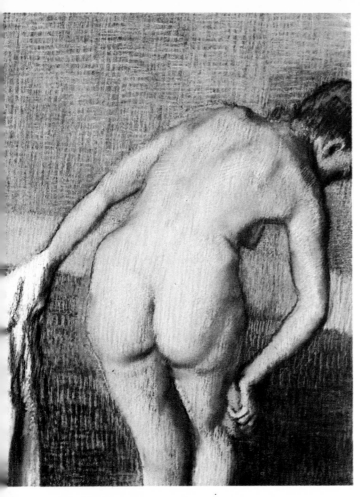

studio depicted scenes from daily life or were sunlit landascapes painted in the open air. They showed colors and lighting effects which no one had dared paint before. None of these fitted into the strictures of academic art. The exhibition itself was an act of revolution, and even more revolutionary were the paintings themselves.

The exhibition created curiosity as well as scandal. The artists were accused of playing a joke on the public simply to draw attention to themselves. A term, coined disdainfully by a journalist in an ironic vein, was adopted by the group as the name of their movement: the Impressionists.

Years of living as outcasts of the official art world passed before these artists were recognized and appreciated. Among them were Monet, Renoir, Pissarro, Sisley, Cézanne, Berthe Morisot, and Degas.

Edgar Degas, the son of Auguste Degas, a banker, decided at twenty to drop his law studies and become an artist. An admirer of Ingres, Degas arranged a meeting with him and declared he wanted to take up a career as a painter. According to Paul Valéry,

Edgar Degas (1834-1917): Woman Bathing *(c. 1886).*
Pastels (28³/₈×22 in.). Private Collection, U.S.

Ingres gave Degas this piece of advice:

Draw lines, my boy, many lines, from memory or from models. That is how you will become a good painter.

Degas did not end up drawing many lines; instead he became one of the principal exponents of Impressionist art. One of his favorite media was pastel. Entire lessons can be learned from his drawings. Let's take a moment and study one.

Look at the reproduction of *Woman Bathing* on the preceding page. You will notice that the pastel is not heavily shaded. Rather, the shading is in the base color. The finishing touches are done with hatching, mostly vertical, a technique, which, in a certain sense, anticipates Pointillism.

A perfectionist, Degas often said:

No art was ever less spontaneous than mine. What I do is the result of reflection and study of the great masters; of inspiration, spontaneity, and temperament, I know nothing.

It is a very good idea to copy what you see, but it is much better to draw what you see only in your memory. It is a transformation in which memory collaborates with imagination. You reproduced only what has struck you, that is, only the necessary things. Here memory and imagination are freed from the tyranny imposed by nature.

(From G. Moore, *Impressions and Opinions*, London, 1891. Chapter on Degas.)

Degas was never satisfied with his work, and he would constantly say:

One must redo the same subject ten, a hundred times. In art, nothing should seem casual, not even movement...

He did not like to sell his art and often refused to exhibit it, adding:

Painting is a private thing, one only works for the few...

To help his brother out of some financial difficulties, Degas was forced to sell several works. By using chalks, he was able to produce some very good works quickly, without having to renounce his high standards or the unusual perspectives he liked.

In his diary, Odilon Redon noted on the subject of Degas's pastels:

What a science of juxtaposed tones, exalted, deliberate, and premeditated, to achieve such fascinating ends!

When I speak about Degas, I always think of one of his best friends, Zandomeneghi, the 19th-century Italian artist.

The Mutton Sleeve by Federico Zandomeneghi

Someday when I have more time, I will try to figure out what happened during 1855 and 1870, between the Macchiaiolists, an Italian movement, and the Impressionists. These two movements came into contact and blended together much more than art historians have hitherto acknowledged.

The great centers like Paris, Milan, and Vienna were so culturally active in these years that it would have been difficult for any artist not to have been influenced by what was going on around him. Paris, especially, held great fascination for those who wanted international experience.

Federico Zandomeneghi was no exception. Born in Venice in 1841, both his father and grandfather were famous sculptors. He enrolled in the Venetian Accademia di Belle Arti at fifteen. In 1859, to avoid conscription in the Austrian army, he fled to Pavia, where he enrolled in the university the next year. Then he joined the Thousand, the expedition led by Garibaldi, and in 1862, he was arrested by the Austrians. When he was released, he fled to Florence where he stayed until 1867. Finally, he left for Paris in 1874, where his political adventures ended and his artistic career began. He went from being a Macchiaiolist to becoming an Impressionist.

In 1878 he set up his studio in the same building as the artists François Gauzi and Toulouse-Lautrec. Toulouse-Lautrec's model, Maria, who was also an artist and the mother of Maurice Utrillo, lived there as well. Gauzi wrote:

Certainly, Lautrec felt his influence: Zando (Zandomeneghi) was the first painter who directed him toward Impressionism. Lautrec adopted his theories immediately and, like him, gave enormous importance to the selection of the visual angle, the positioning of his subject on paper, and how the subject would seem to extend beyond the frame of the painting...

Zandomeneghi was also close to Renoir and a great friend of Degas. From him, Zandomeneghi learned how to use perspective, following the Impressionists' rules, which, to the artist, suggested life in action. Some figures were cut off at the waistline, while others were painted with their faces partially cut off by the frame. He, more than the others, concentrated on images that "went on," suggesting a continuation of life beyond the picture frame.

Federico Zandomeneghi (1841-1917): The Mutton Sleeve. *Pastel (19³/₄ × 15³/₄ in.). Private Collection, Milan.*

Although Zandomeneghi was well regarded in Paris during his lifetime, he was virtually unknown in Italy. In 1914, he exhibited at the Biennale, in Venice, and as usual, received a lukewarm reception. His art was too modern, too frank, too independent, and too difficult to please the lazy and cautious official critics as well as the not very enlightened public. Zandomeneghi commented on the event:

Not a single old friend has written a word about my exhibition, which proves they did not like it. There is no reason to go back to Italy just to feel sorry for myself...

He died in Paris in 1917, three months after his friend Degas.

Look now at the half-portrait of a woman reproduced here, and let us see how he created it.

He began by drawing the figure in charcoal, over which he superimposed pastels, using diagonal strokes.

Observe carefully how the range of blues gives the whole drawing a truly extraordinary quality of fullness. Even the flesh tones have a soft, bluish film. A light tone was probably spread first, the color then blended with a finger, followed by hatching on top. The lights in her dress were obtained with a red pastel identical to that used for the skin.

Now, notice the composition of this work. The half-portrait fits into an equilateral triangle, whose points are at the top of her head, her elbow, and the lower part of her back. The figure seems to continue on beyond the edges of the paper.

Let us now see how to do a pastel in Zandomeneghi's style.

Drawing a Portrait

On the following page is a portrait I sketched of my mother holding a guitar in 1986, using a gray, Canson-type paper. Remember, even the color of the paper is important when you are doing pastels.

Let us analyze the different steps that make up this drawing.

First, I sketched in the figure with a sanguine chalk, and then traced the contours of the arm with sepia. This was done to create greater contrast and accentuate the roundness of the flesh.

After the contouring, I drew the dress, varying the blues from very cool tones in the foreground to a slightly warmer, greenish blue in the middle ground.

I drew the face and neck with dabs of similar colored chalks, using warmer or cooler

tones according to the distance and volume I wanted to create (cooler for the parts in the shadows and warmer for the areas in the light).

Then I smudged it with my finger and repeated the same operation with the hair. Afterward, I sprayed it lightly to form a color base and accented the background colors around the contours.

If you look closely at the arm in the foreground, you may be able to see more clearly the process I followed. First, I went over the arm once with a layer of color, blending the tones of the dress with those of the arm. This gave a cool shadowed effect up to the elbow. Then, I used this as a base for the rest of the portrait.

Let us see now, step by step, how to do a figure using sanguine chalk.

Sketching the Figure with Sanguine Chalk

You should start with your model sitting down, letting him or her assume a natural, comfortable position. This way, the model will be able to keep a pose longer. Try to fit several studies on the same sheet of paper.

So you can vary the play of light as much as you like, use a lamp which can be moved easily as a source of light for your model. Sketch the figure, trying to imagine the anatomical structure hidden under the clothing. Remember that you must know how to construct the body, or your figure will be out of proportion or, worse, end up looking like a sack of potatoes.

Andrea del Sarto (1486-1551): Two Studies for "Hanging Captains". *Sanguine (10³/₄×5 in.). Uffizi Gallery, Florence.*

97

For example, look at the figures by Andrea del Sarto on page 97. They will give you a better idea of how you should proceed.

To construct the basic figure, follow the rules of construction explained in the preceding sections on drawing anatomy. You can also refer back to what I taught you about drawing a bowl of eggs—that is, you should also draw the part that is not seen. As we know from studying the great masters, nothing is left to chance. In fact, in their work, the more carefully constructed a design is, the more it appears to be instinctive. Their work is carefully planned to look casual. Even when an artist shows only part of the figure, the whole effect is calculated ahead of time.

Look at the portrait reproduced here. As usual, I started with the head, and then I went on to outline the geometric structure—just as I showed you when we did the still life exercises.

The upper figure on the left was outlined first. Then I shaded it by using the palm of my hand to rub light strokes of color. The lower figure on the right, I sketched with the side of the crayon making broad strokes, outlining and shading at the same time to form the shaded areas and add volume. I do not advise you to try this immediately, though. It is better just to indicate them lightly, filling them in gradually and letting them develop in relation to the lighter areas and the halftones.

I cannot repeat often enough the importance of basic construction in a drawing. Do not let yourself become self-indulgent; you should always do the very best you can. It is the only way to become a true professional.

I guarantee that if you work hard, you will never be bored. In fact, each time you have

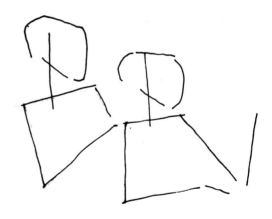

finished a drawing, you should find yourself wanting to improve it by doing another.

99

My Son Andrea, Done in Sanguine

To pin down my son Andrea to pose for me has been a herculean task, like trying to pick up a drop of mercury on the floor.

The construction of the drawing on the left has been colored over, but I want to describe the method in order to remind you how important positioning the model is. I did the basic sketch very quickly; then I worked on the drawing in six basic stages.

First, I defined the angle of the head and, following the relationship I explained to you before, outlined the construction. Next I drew the upper torso and arms, then the hands.

At this point I went back to the head, filling in the details and defining the eyes, nose, and ears. Then I went on to the figure, concentrating on the folds in his sweater. I continued with the details of his hand and fingers and finally filled in the general shading and other details.

I did another study of Andrea during this same period. This time he was asleep on the sofa. Obviously, this drawing, as you can imagine, was easier, while the one reproduced here was much more demanding. So

Right, Andrea Maiotti: Copy of a Plaster Bust. *Sanguine.*

much so, in fact, that it was the last time I ever drew him.

Andrea is now fifteen and attends one of the top art schools in Milan. He, in his turn, has become a good draftsman. If he gives himself wholeheartedly to his work, his skill will provide him with a lot of satisfaction.

On the preceding page look at the drawing of a plaster cast Andrea made using sanguine chalk. All of the blending was done using the chalk on its side.

You might find it useful to get hold of some classical plaster busts to copy. Such exercises are indispensable to one's artistic development.

Of course, you will need somewhere to keep them. One solution might be to rent a studio with several other people. Look for places you can fix up: half-abandoned old buildings on the outskirts of town or attics in old houses. Arrange the space so you can work in the middle of a room and leave the walls free for hanging up your works and storing the plaster casts and other objects you want to copy.

Luisella—A Portrait in Charcoal

My wife, Luisella, is my favorite model, perhaps because she is always willing to pose. I drew this portrait of her immediately after we had returned home from an exhibition of works by Edvard Munch, the Norwegian artist (some of whose drawings I have already shown you on previous pages).

Seeing Munch's paintings and graphics inspired me so much that I was not able to go to bed until I had finished the portrait.

For this portrait, I used a mixed technique. With the edge of a piece of charcoal, I outlined the contours, and then holding it flat, I filled in the basic shadows.

After lightly spraying with fixative, I dusted it with a brush. I then went back over the lines and shadows and finished with more fixative. The last step was hatching, done in long strokes, with a piece of charcoal $3/4$ inch thick.

This "mixed" technique gives the drawing a freshness found only in smaller sketches.

Portrait of Giambologna by Hendrick Goltzius

The drawing reproduced on page 104 by a great master of the past bears the inscription: *Giovan de Bolonia Beelthoower tot florencen ghenconterf... H. Goltzius 1591*. It portrays Giambologna, the Florentine sculptor of Flemish origin.

Hendrick Goltzius (1558-1617):
Giambologna. *Charcoal and sanguine*
(14^1/$_2$ × 11^3/$_4$ in.). Teylers Museum,
Haarlem.

The portrait was done by Goltzius in Florence when the artist was preparing to return to Holland. Goltzius was a very refined Dutch artist and engraver, who was born in 1558 and died in 1617.

He came to Italy in 1590-91 and spent time in Florence, Venice, and Rome, where he studied ancient sculpture, drawing, and paintings by Raphael, Parmigianino, and the Venetian 16th-century masters.

Note the chromatic effect he obtained using charcoal and sanguine. The torso was sketched in charcoal with broad strokes while the face was drawn with sanguine. The details are a combination of the two. Black is added only in the darkest areas—the nostrils, for example, and the left side of the nose, as we face it, and the upper eyelid. The detailed work on the hair, eyebrows, and beard, done with a hard, sharp piece of charcoal, is very fine indeed. His moustache, as you can see, has been very delicately shaded with the sanguine.

Detail of a Face Drawn with Sanguine

Here I have sketched the eye of one of my friends, using both a sanguine pencil and a charcoal pencil.

It is important to remember, when doing a detail like this, to work with just the tip of your pencil. This means you will be constantly sharpening it.

I have divided the eye into two parts, giving the left side more detail, while leaving the right side somewhat sketchy.

Beginning with the eye, try drawing some details of faces yourself. Ask friends or family members to pose for you.

Shade the eye following the examples reproduced on previous pages. Draw them facing you or in three-quarters profile. You

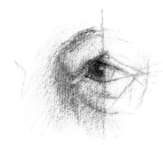

should make the basic lines and outline the shadows with very light, almost imperceptible hatching.

Now fill in the shadows and the iris with

Giovanni Antonio Boltraffio (1467-1516): left, Portrait of Saint Barbara. *Charcoal and sanguine (21''×16 in.). Right,* Portrait a Man. *Charcoal and sanguine (21¹/₈×16 in.). Pinacoteca Ambrosiana, Milan.*

delicate cross-hatching, using a sanguine pencil. Spray the drawing with fixative, then concentrate on the darkest shadows. Work lightly with the charcoal. Aim for maximum shadow, going over it two or three times with the charcoal. Do not be in a hurry to finish it.

Two Charcoal and Sanguine Chalk Portraits by Giovanni Antonio Boltraffio

Boltraffio was born in Milan in 1467 and died in 1516. He was fifteen when he entered Leonardo da Vinci's workshop.

Of Leonardo da Vinci's students, he was without question the most outstanding. He was so good one might even imagine master and pupil collaborating on some works.

The two drawings reproduced here are important for their very high quality and for the technical expertise they demonstrate.

Leonardo da Vinci's circle understood drawing as an area of experimentation. These two portraits are good examples of works that used a mixed technique.

The paper was probably treated with an animal glue and colored with a little ocher. The drawing was done in charcoal with touches of lead point, sanguine, and sepia. Highlights have been added with white lead.

The portrait of the woman has traditionally been thought to be one of Isabella of Aragon, wife of Gian Galeazzo Visconti. The identity of the man has not been established for certain, though there have been many theories about it.

A Profile of Isabella

I did the portrait of my daughter Isabella on the following page, using charcoal, pastel crayons, and a chalk base on cover stock.

Why don't you try a similar portrait? First, look for a model similar to Isabella. Have her sit very straight, almost regally, in a hard-backed chair. Sketch with a very soft piece of charcoal beginning with an outline of the head, then spread a delicate background of charcoal over the areas that will be in shadow. For the face and neck, you should use light ocher and then go over the shadows with natural umber. Pick out the parts of the face that have higher colors, such as the cheeks and the tip of the nose, and give them a slight reddish tinge with burnt sienna.

The hair should be done with charcoal, while the blouse is colored with a light red in the highlighted areas and cobalt violet in the darkest areas. Using a white pastel crayon,

108

highlight the background, the tip of her nose, her cheekbone, and her shoulder—all the areas that catch the most light.

Speaking of light, remember to pay attention to the play of light and shadow when you decide where to place your lamp. Try several positions, moving both model and lamp, before you make your final choice. Selecting the way shadows fall is an important part of a good drawing. You should not underestimate it.

Isabella is my oldest child. Like Andrea, she also goes to an art school. Her artistic talent and sensitivity is demonstrated in the drawing I have reproduced on the right.

It is a copy of a classic plaster bust that she drew with some of the same techniques I use for my pastel drawings. Her's is a very clean-lined technique, and the hatching shows a great confidence.

Alone! by Emilio Longoni

Before I tell you about the artist who did the pastel on page 111, I would like you to look at it closely. Enjoy the marvelous chromatic qualities he created using Pointillist techniques.

As I noted before, the technique of pastels is not unlike that of Pointillism. In fact, if you look at a pastel closely, you will see many short, colored strokes that will remind you of Pointillist strokes. The exponents of this artistic movement believed that a color

Isabella Maiotti: Copy of a Plaster Bust. *Pastel.*

obtained by mixing two pure colors together was less bright and clear than the same color obtained by putting two pure tints side by side and letting the eye fuse them.

Emilio Longoni was born in Barlassina, near Milan, in 1859. Of humble origin, he attended night school at the Accademia di Brera in Milan. He and Segantini, another Italian artist, were given contracts with the merchant and painter Vittore Grubicy de Dragon in 1880. Until 1893 he worked closely with Segantini. A falling out with Grubicy, who apparently had persuaded Segantini to sign one of Longoni's works, put an end to the friendship.

Longoni was considered the anarchists' artist. Like the Impressionists, the Macchiaiolists, and the movements that followed them, most of Longoni's works had social themes.

This wonderful pastel shows the figure of a woman caught in a moment of great despair. The position of the body and the hands, the interior light, the light outside, the reflection on the table, and the placement of the flowers and candle in the foreground, all contribute to create an atmosphere of profound sadness and solitude.

These were the social themes Longoni worked with. This poor woman, with her hands clasped heartrendingly in prayer, expresses deep pain, capturing the emotions of the spectator and making him share in it.

Note his confident use of Pointillist technique; he makes green by placing dashes of blue and yellow next to each other, and the violet tone from dashes of blue and red.

Besides its technique, this pastel is also noteworthy for its composition. Longoni was another artist who left nothing to chance.

Portrait of a Woman by Umberto Boccioni

The pastel on page 112 was done by Boccioni in 1909. In it we can see how the principles of Pointillism were transformed into something more dynamic.

The life of this artist could be defined as dynamic as well. Along with painters Giacomo Balla, Carlo Carrà, Luigi Russolo, and Gino Severini, he signed the *Manifesto of Futurist Painters* in February 1910.

I found several of the excerpts from this manifesto, as well as others from the *Technical Manifesto of Futurist Painting*, rather interesting, especially for the conclusions they reached.

Emilio Longoni (1859-1932): Alone! *(1900). Pastel.*
(25³/₅×49¹/₅ in.). Casa di Lavoro e Patronato per i Ciechi
di Guerra della Lombardia, Milan.

Umberto Boccioni (1882-1916): Portrait of a Woman *(1909). Pastel (21^1/$_4$×22^7/$_{16}$ in.). Private Collection, Verona.*

From the *Manifesto of Futurist Painters*:
To the young artists of Italy! it begins, and then it goes on: *Living art draws its life from the surrounding environment. Our forebears drew their artistic inspiration from a religious atmosphere, which fed their souls; in the same way we must breathe in the tangible miracles of contemporary life—the iron network of speedy communications which envelops the earth, the transatlantic liners, the* Dreadnoughts, *those marvelous flights which furrow our skies, the profound courage of our submarine navigators, and the spasmodic struggle to conquer the unknown...*

We will also play our part in this crucial revival of aesthetic expression: we declare war on all artists and all institutions which insist on hiding behind a facade of false modernity, while they are actually ensnared by tradition, academicism and, above all, a nauseating cerebral laziness...

These are our final conclusions:
With our enthusiastic adherence to Futurism, we will:
1. Destroy the cult of the past, the obsession with the ancients, pedantry, and academic formalism.
2. Totally invalidate all kinds of imitation.
3. Elevate all attempts at originality, however daring, however violent.
4. Bear bravely and proudly the smear of "madness" with which they try to gag all innovators.
5. Regard art critics as useless and dangerous.
6. Rebel against the tyranny of words: "harmony" and "good taste," loose expressions which can be used to destroy the works of Rembrandt, Goya, and Rodin.
7. Sweep the whole field of art clean of all themes and subjects which have been used in the past.
8. Support and glory in our day-to-day world, a world which is going to be continually and splendidly transformed by victorious science.

The dead shall be buried in the earth's deepest bowels! The threshold of the future will be swept free of mummies! Make room for youth, for violence, for daring!

The preoccupation with movement was a constant feature of Futurism, but for Boccioni it assumed a special importance, and the depiction of the "dynamic sensation" became the focus of his art.

In the *Technical Manifesto of Futurist Painting* he wrote:

All things move, all things run, all things are rapidly changing. A profile is never motionless before our eyes, but it constantly appears and disappears. On account of the persistency of an image upon the retina, moving objects constantly multiply themselves; their form changes like rapid vibrations, in their mad career. Thus a running horse has not four legs, but twenty, and their movements are triangular.

All is conventional in art. Nothing is absolute in painting. What was truth for the painters of yesterday is but a falsehood today.

We declare, for instance, that a portrait must not be like the sitter, and that the painter carries in himself the landscapes which he would fix upon his canvas. To paint a human figure you must not paint it; you must render the whole of its surrounding atmosphere.

Space no longer exists: the street pavement, soaked by rain beneath the glare of electric lamps, becomes immensely deep and gapes to the very center of the earth. Thousands of miles divide us from the sun; yet the house in front of us fits into the solar disk.

Who can still believe in the opacity of bodies, since our sharpened and multiplied sensitiveness has already penetrated the obscure manifestations of the medium? Why should we forget in our creations the doubled power of our sight, capable of giving results analogous to those of the X rays?

These statements accurately reflect Boccioni's character, and this drawing, one of the many pastels the artist made, does too. Unfortunately, his life was cut short in 1916 when, at the age of 34, he died following a fall from a horse. Ironically, he died, not in the thick of battle, but on a routine military exercise with his cavalry regiment.

The *Portrait of a Woman* was done in charcoal and smudged with a finger. The effect of the colored lights was achieved using a technique that vaguely recalls Pointillism. Most of the colors which Boccioni used are cool, and they contrast with the soft, warm tones of the figure and the wall.

Through the window, one can see horses in a meadow that has been colored with white, veronese green, yellow ocher, and cerulean blue. This tonality gives us the sensation of being inside the room, looking out through the window. If you observe carefully, you will note the glass in the window also affects the way the light falls on the woman's face.

Vincent Van Gogh as Portrayed by Toulouse-Lautrec

Henri-Marie-Raymond de Toulouse-Lautrec-Monfa—for that was his full name—was born in Albi in 1864 and is said to have given indication of his artistic vocation even as a child.

I once read somewhere that when he was three, he asked to sign his brother's baptismal certificate. When we was told he could not, because he did not know how to write, he replied: *Then I will draw an ox on it.*

Toulouse-Lautrec had a highly developed artistic sense and would probably have become an artist in any case, but two falls from horses made him deformed for the rest of his life. These accidents and their results probably played a strong role in his becoming a serious artist.

By the age of seventeen he had decided that art would indeed be his lifework. His first teacher was René Priceteau, a friend of his father's, who specialized in painting dogs and horses. Later he entered the studio of Léon Bonnat, an academic painter much in vogue at the time.

Toulouse-Lautrec wrote to his uncle Charles:

Perhaps you would be interested to know what sort of encouragement Bonnat gives me. He tells me: "Your painting is not bad, a bit ingenuous perhaps, but all together not bad. Your drawing, on the other hand, is really dreadful." I must take my courage in both hands and start again...

Toulouse-Lautrec studied with Bonnat conscientiously, despite his personal inclinations. In 1882, he went on to study with Fernand Cormon, a poor but cheerful academic painter. In Cormon's studio, Toulouse-Lautrec met artists who would come to play decisive roles in his life, expanding his horizons, and encouraging his antiacademic tendencies.

Toulouse-Lautrec loved the works of Velázquez, Goya, Ingres, and Renoir. He particularly admired Degas, who provided him with forms of composition, which he freely adapted in a simpler and more audacious fashion and with a whole new repertory of contemporary subjects. Like all the Impressionists, he was also fascinated with Japanese prints. At the time many artists were attracted to this style, but they used only the elements that suited them and Toulouse-Lautrec was no exception.

He was a great friend of all the Impressionists, including van Gogh. He drew the

*Henry de Toulouse-Lautrec (1864-
1901):* Portrait of van Gogh at the
Café *(1887). Pastel (22¹/₂ × 18¹/₂ in.).
V. van Gogh Collection, Laren.*

fine pastel of his Dutch friend on straw-colored paper. Notice how the short strokes give the whole drawing a spiral movement. The background is formed by a play of emerald green, ultramarine blue, cobalt violet, yellows, yellow-orange, and reds. The two tables and the figure also contain several lighter shades of blue and a lot of yellow, red, and green, while the dominant colors of the face are yellow and white. The drawing was made with only a few colors, and later Toulouse-Lautrec would modify and perfect this technique.

Vincent van Gogh met Toulouse-Lautrec in 1886 in Cormon's studio, where they both worked. Toulouse-Lautrec admired the works and ideas of this stubborn, taciturn Dutchman, who seemed almost happy in his solitude. This pastel portrait of van Gogh comes from this period. Two years later, when van Gogh was growing tired of living in Paris, Toulouse-Lautrec suggested that he spend some time in the southeast of France where he himself had spent part of his childhood. After van Gogh left, the two artists only saw each other again on one occasion— when van Gogh made a short trip to Paris. Two weeks later the painter of *Sunflowers* and *Starry Night* put a tragic end to his life.

A Portrait with Pastel Pencils

Wax-based pastels are most often used by graphic artists and illustrators. For the portrait on the next page, I worked on sepia-colored paper and shaded in a white background with a chalk pastel.

First, I drew the model (in this case, my wife) with a sanguine pencil. A white pencil would have created too violent a contrast with the dark paper. I also could have used a red, green, or blue pencil—as long as they were light in tone.

For the shadows I tried to take advantage of the background color of the paper as much as possible.

A few strokes of yellow ocher were used to draw the hair in the areas that received indirect light. Cross-hatching filled in the areas where the most light fell, while ultramarine-blue cross-hatching created the half-shadows, giving the hair a luminous depth. I used the same colors for the face but superimposed a vermilion red on the warmest parts, the cheekbones, nose, and lips. To emphasize the shadow under the nose, I used cerulean blue instead of ultramarine.

The dress is a blend of carmine red, vermilion red, and white.

Three Portraits by Gianni Maimeri

How can one best use the same model for different portraits? On this and the following pages you will find three examples.

Maimeri portrayed the same model in three different poses to create these lovely pastels. In all of them, the model is his wife. Notice what she is wearing helps to establish a particular mood. Keep in mind that along with the background of the drawing, the composition, and the position of the model, it is important to decide how your model should be dressed. The colors of the dress should be the ones you use in your painting. You should always pay a great deal of attention to the combinations, affinities, and especially the clashes of colors. This is a crucial element in the artist's bag of tricks.

Let us read more from Maimeri's notes on color theory and see what he has to say about its importance:

There are, we have seen, different ways to look at color.

In his perception of the physical characteristics of colors, the painter is no different from the dyer. With enough practice, anyone can acquire the ability to perceive gradations of color and the play of reflections. A trained eye can see the colors of objects in the at-

Gianni Maimeri: Portrait of a Woman *(c. 1920). Pastel (27$^1/_2$ × 19$^3/_4$ in.). Private Collection.*

119

mosphere with an exactness that the ordinary person cannot. The latter can only recognize the true color of an object through the veil of colored light with which the atmosphere blankets it.

In the same way, the attentive observer is not fooled by the tricks of perspective, which can deform perpendicular projections on inclined planes.

But all these processes only involve the way we look at things; so far, they do not involve art.

In every problem related to aesthetics, the question of the relationship between reality and subjectivity always comes up.

When we are speaking of a reality as essential as that of color, this relantionship is basic, for no visual reality is conceivable without color. The question then is: How does it influence and transform a work of art?

The ability to achieve a certain result by combining two or more physical facts from the same category (light vibrations, for example) derives from human nature rather than from the laws of physics. And this inevitably means diversity in the way each individual understands that phenomenon. Each person sees things in his own way, and this can be easily proven by giving various people the ex-

Gianni Maimeri: Portrait of a Woman (c. 1920). Pastel (27¹/₂×19³/₄ in.). Private Collection.

act same palette of paint; each person will see the colors differently.

But we are still not talking about art. So far, we are closer to taste, personal biases, or psychology. It is true that certain colors (and I am speaking here of real, visible colors and also certain zones of optical colors) have similar meanings for most people. Thus, if we go through the color spectrum, the fact that red produces a higher number of measurable vibrations may be why it is so often associated with fire (since fire is not only red). The ambiguity of lemon yellow may be linked to its median position in the spectrum, as well as the rareness with which it is found in nature in its pure form. It certainly cannot compete with the shininess of gold, for example, and next to the magic of green it looks quite harsh. Look at blue. The idea of its sanctity surely comes from the blue of the heavens, while the subtle poisons of violet and purple recall the colors of the sunset and of death.

Rosen Sthile has analyzed the color base of many objects. The warmest ones, the ones we most like to surround ourselves with, have a color base similar to that of flesh.

Art only becomes a reality when the painter's idea is translated into the appropriate medium, which in its turn ex-

Gianni Maimeri: Portrait of a Woman (c. 1920). Pastel (27¹/₂ × 19³/4 in.). Private Collection.

121

presses itself through the palette.

The painter, both from his natural inclinations and interests and the means at his disposal, begins to create a palette of colors with which he will come to identify, referring to it for every visual representation he undertakes. For the painter, there are no longer colored objects as such, only objects which are the result of a mixture of paints. What might be a lovely flower for you, the source of an idea or emotion, is for me an agreement reached between lacquer red, sky blue, white, and yellow, cooled with a touch of emerald. Yet, at the same time, it is still a flower. Where you see the pure sky become dark with the heavy fumes of pollution from the earth below, I see orange, tempered with white, flickering between blue-greens and purples.

You see, for a painter there is not one color, but three: a primary color, its complement, and the almost neutral base which completes it. The Pointillists have had a tremendous influence on painting.

The error of theoreticians has been to try to find laws in objective reality and physics when we should be looking at sensation and sentiment.

Every painter has his own kind of Pointillism which is infallible and right for him.

To be aware of this is, for me, to be making notable progress in understanding the psychological phenomena that accompany art.

A native art does not exist, except with certain metaphysicists and aesthetic mystics. Art, and thus painting, is above all, knowledge in the full sense of the word. It is not ability or abstract cognizance. This knowledge is lateral, but it is still linked to a single means, to the practical search for technique. It is a quest that is enriching, even though it is often slow and tiring.

One is not born with a ready-made language of painting, nor is color instinctive.

The colors used in painting, a three-way agreement between subjective expression, experience, and the objective equivalent of feeling, are not acquired except after long consideration, long usage of color, infinitive comparisons, and obstinacy.

This can be seen with the young, who may seem to be colorists, but are really tonalists. Look at how quickly a child acquires a sense of objective, abstract color before he learns to see color in its visual reality. He is like someone blind from birth who suddenly sees color for the first time. The blind man who finally sees would be the perfect tonalist because he would have a fresh, unaffected vision. But he would not yet be a painter because color would have no emotional meaning for him.

For us, it is only when color takes on a personality and this personality wraps itself around our emotional life that a material manifestation of it takes on the proper resonance and turns into a system of rules (even if this is only subconscious). Only then do we have the conditions for understanding pictorial truths.

In this sense, many pictures are of only transient interest. Even when they are painted in the colors of the peacock, they are still only geese. I will try to show later how the great works of art, even when they do not flaunt their use of color, have their origins here, as does every pictorial work.

This is because form is not opposed to color. The two are not parallel concepts, and it impossible to choose between one and the other, as some attempt to do. Color (and I am still speaking of color in art) must envelope, symbolize, and make up form (in other words, a thought); there is no form if it does not contain color.

It would be like saying that a sound is not rhythmic and a rhythm has no sound.

* * *

Any new system of precepts would be rejected out of hand as cumbersome and restrictive if it were represented as though it were absolute.

What can be useful and true about it, though, are the new ideas it carries within it. These are often ahead of their time, and are introduced by someone who, rather like the town crier of the past, heralds their coming. Yet he has not invented them from nothing. There had to be at least a kernel of an idea floating around, if not a whole system.

This system is both a critical analysis and history.

As critical analysis, it makes order out of new ideas, finding new relationships and connections. As history, it records and documents the psychological phenomena that the "town crier" has announced.

This is the sense in which its selectivity and discrimination is useful to us.

A system of precepts cannot solve any aesthetic or practical problem concerning art. If, along the centuries, the human thought has indeed come to limit and distinguish art from all other spiritual manifestations, it still remains a matter which goes beyond any definition, since it has its sources in the most undefinable core of the human self.

Portrait of a Girl by Gustav Klimt

I chose this portrait because I was struck by its sweetness and the tender feelings it evokes. It is hard to believe this is the same Gustav Klimt who created all those sensual portraits of women. Klimt always loved drawing the female figure. His sequence of portraits of women that were such an important part of his work testify to this.

Klimt was born in Austria in 1862 and died in 1918. Following a family tradition, he enrolled in the School of Arts and Crafts in Vienna, where he learned a wide range of techniques. This helped him understand how all the visual arts are related—an understanding that became the starting point for his future experiments. The desire for renewal, the eagerness to try new forms, and the ever more pervasive use of symbolism constantly appear in his work.

Consider this portrait of a young girl. It was made with very few colors: the color of the paper, gradations of white pastels, a delicate red, and charcoal.

To understand this man better, let us read what another young artist, Egon Schiele, had to say about him:

The first time I went to see Klimt, I found a thickset man with a tanned face and harsh

Gustav Klimt (1862-1918): Portrait of a Girl *(1902). Pastel (17³/₄ × 12³/₈ in.). Historisches Museum der Stadt Wien.*

124

features. I met him at number 21, Josefstädterstrasse, in his garden—one of those old hidden gardens that still exist in the Josefstadt, the kind which lie in front of a small, low house with lots of windows and are shaded by very tall trees. A path among flowers and creepers led to the house, and one entered through a glass door into a vestibule where a pile of stretched canvases and other painting materials were stacked. From there one passed on to a series of three connecting studios, were hundreds of sketches were scattered on the floor. Klimt always wore a large, blue smock that reached down to his feet, and he met everyone, visitors and models alike, wearing this outfit.

The neighborhood was torn down in 1911, and Klimt, forced to leave his little house among all the greenery where he had spent so many years of joy and sorrow, moved to a single-story house in Feldmühlgasse in Hietzing. It had two large windows on the north side of the house, and Klimt picked out the room which they lighted, arranging it as his work area. Everyday, after breakfast at the Tivoli, he returned home to paint and draw uninterrupted from ten in the morning until eight at night.

Sunday morning he was to be found walking around Mödling and Baden. Every year he rearranged the flower beds around his house. It was so pleasant to arrive there among the profusion of flowers and leafy trees. Two pretty heads, which Klimt had sculpted himself, stood on each side of the entrance. This opened onto a foyer from which by a door on the left, one entered the sitting room. It was furnished with a square table in the center and a large number of Japanese woodcuts covering the wall, along with two larger Chinese paintings. African sculpture stood here and there on the floor, and in the corner closest to the window was a red and black Japanese weapon. From here one went on to two other rooms that looked out over a rose garden. If you went through the door to the right of the foyer, you entered a bedroom with two beds and through it to another. The back wall of this room was entirely covered by an enormous wardrobe, containing a collection of splendid Chinese and Japanese clothing. The room led to the studio where Klimt showed me what he was working on... His generous nature was genuine. He was no hermit, in fact he was quite cordial. Still, he knew who his real friends were. He earned quite a lot of money and he spent every cent of it. "Money should circulate," he said.

Four Portrait Studies

Continuing with our study of the figure, let us look at how to draw a fully dressed figure. For a more accurate study, I suggest you work with either sanguine or charcoal. Working with only one color will help you learn how to combine the different elements of the drawing into a whole.

I have chosen two charcoal drawings of my mother, which I painted twenty years apart, one in 1965 and the other in 1985, and two drawings by van Gogh.

Around 1970, I was very interested in van Gogh; inspired by his work, I had many of my models assume the same positions as his models. (Do not forget the importance of position when you pose your model.)

To study an artist—and this is important for anyone who is going to become one—does not mean to copy him. Instead, it means trying to see as he does, imagining yourself in his world, reading everything you can find about him, including the notes or writing he left, even using the same materials as he did to express yourself.

Observe van Gogh's charcoal drawing, *The Gleaner*, which he did in one sitting, most likely in the open air.

The strokes are broad and spontaneous,

Vincent van Gogh (1853-1890): The Gleaner *(1885). Charcoal ($16^3/_8 \times 12^1/_2$ in.). Museum Folkwang, Essen.*

126

done in one draft, as artists were accustomed to doing then.

Notice how the strokes follow the movement of the dress and the roundness of the body, arms, and head. They seem casually to capture the impression of an instant, and at the same time, the emotion of a great painting.

Let us go back now to my drawings. The first one, which portrays my mother sitting while she sews, I did with black charcoal on white wrapping paper. You will see that the stool is only lightly sketched, while the figure is first outlined and then shaded. I did this using the edge of the charcoal.

Now, move on to the charcoal drawing I made twenty years later and reproduced on the following page. You will immediately note the physical changes which have occurred with the passage of time. Her figure is rounder, and her attitude is less active, more tranquil and contemplative. I often see her with her hands in her lap, gazing off into the distance, with an enigmatic expression on her face, like the cat at her side. For this drawing I used a very thick charcoal stick on cover stock. Note the composition. Behind the figure, next to a chain fence which has some ivy growing on it, is the trunk of a

peach tree. Above her you can see the leaves of the tree.

Now look at van Gogh's other sketch done with blue and green pastels, a very daring choice of colors.

Before beginning work with these two colors (which possibly were the only two he had, given his economic problems) he must have carefully analyzed his subject and divided it into two areas, light and shadow.

Of the two colors he chose, the green worked better in the areas where the light fell, while the blue served best for the shadows. Looking at the way these two colors were used and the effect they produce, one guesses that the light on his model was coming from a gas lamp.

I recently read that one of van Gogh's paintings was sold for millions of dollars. I cannot help but think of the life of privation that van Gogh suffered and how he never had enough money to pay his models or buy supplies. Van Gogh was a good and generous man, but with the deprivations and disappointments of his life, another stubborn, even violent side emerged over the years. One result of this was the traumatic fight he had with Paul Gauguin, who had joined him in Arles. The two artists shared a little

Vincent van Gogh: The Violinist *(1886). Pastel (12¹/₂ × 10¹/₄ in.). Rijksmuseum Vincent van Gogh, Amsterdam.*

house that van Gogh called "the house of friends." Van Gogh looked up to Gauguin as an artist, but at the same time, he wanted to affirm his own personality, displaying the technical discoveries he had made and the new confidence he felt, coming from his experiments. One night a fight developed between the two artists, and van Gogh attacked Gauguin twice with a razor. In an act of self-punishment and mortification, van Gogh cut off one of his ears. Not long after, he painted a self-portrait showing his bandaged head.

The French painter Emile Bernard wrote in the preface to the *Letters of Vincent Van Gogh* (1911):

A painter he is, and a painter he will remain—as a young man translating the brown tones of Holland, later as an adult, when as a Pointillist he painted Montmartre and its gardens, and finally in the Midi or Auvers-sur-Oise, where he painted with such fury. Whether he drew or not, whether he lost himself in little dabs of paint or in deformations, he was always a painter. It is this, together with the rare harmony he sometimes found in a combination of tones, that makes him worthy of our attention and that places him in the top rank of temperamental artists.

A Seated Figure

The next pastel, a portrait of my wife, is another one done with only a few colors. Here is how I did it.

First, I constructed the figure, using a sepia-colored pastel for the outline and shaping the shadows in the basic construction, which was the foundation.

The other colors were reduced to the essential: a few touches of yellow ocher where the light falls on the skin, a bit of vermilion red in the warm areas of the figure, and white smudged with a finger over the sepia base to create a thin, graysh cast to the sweater. Then I sprayed it with fixative and put in the final, white highlights.

A useful exercise for you would be to make a drawing and then dust it lightly with a brush so that only a slight trace of it remains. Then go back over it, retracing lines and shadows as you keep referring back to your subject.

When you do this exercise, close your eyes and force yourself to memorize the image, then open your eyes and draw what you remember. Continue the exercise until you can also fill in the colors from memory.

The first few times you do this, it will seem rather difficult, but as you gain experience, you will gradually begin to develop your visual memory, and once you have it, you will never lose it.

When you have developed this skill, and you see something you would like to draw, the image will stick in your mind. Later you will be able to go back and draw it from memory.

Repeat this exercise as often as possible, and you will develop an unusual mastery of it. I think you will also find it an amusing challenge, as you begin to notice things that others do not pick up. Eventually you will have such a file of shapes and images in your memory that you will be able to draw anything, from a poppy to a bicycle, from a sailboat on a lake to a horse. You will no longer need a model sitting in front of you. You will be able to draw from the storehouse of pictures in your mind. Another challenging exercise is to draw a figure from memory, concentrating on how the light would fall. Then have someone pose in the same position as the figure you remember, with the light falling the same way, and check to see how close you come.

Always strive for perfection, even when you are trying to draw from memory. And remember that few people are completely

satisfied with their children, but they still love them. It is the love that is important, and it must be given without reserve. Art is like that, too—at least that is the way I look at it.

A Ballerina by Edgar Degas

Degas became friendly with musicians, orchestra leaders, and other people at the Paris Opéra. There, behind the scenes, he discovered a world of subjects to portray. Besides the musicians, he also drew the audience sitting in their boxes, sometimes putting in one of his friends, like the banker Hecht or the engraver Lepic. Attached to the theater was the ballet school, where the director of the Opéra trained groups of young dancers nicknamed "rats," which Degas frequently visited.

Around 1872, he traveled to America with his brother René and stopped in New Orleans. His mother had been born there, and he had two brothers working in the cotton business. He returned to France in 1873, and in the autumn of that year, the Opera House burned down, depriving him for a while of his favorite subjects. But the dancing school moved to a new site, and Degas began once again to depict his beloved "rats," the dancing master, and the Opéra musicians.

Degas studied the movement of his subjects and the precise discipline, which was the result of rigorous practice. Dancing, like art, allows for no error, bound as it is to rules. By now, Degas had developed the habit of photographing in his mind the subjects which interested him—dancers or horses or whatever. He would make quick notes or a few sketches to help his memory and then work on them in his studio. This was just the opposite of what his contemporaries were doing; they preferred to work with their subject directly in front of them.

Study this little dancer, this lovely "rat." Look at how she is weighed down with tension. Using only a few colors, the play of white smudged with a finger and black to outline the figure, Degas has brought to life an impression he stored in his memory. The other colors he chose are part of another sort of memory, perhaps chosen for their chromatic effect.

Edgar Degas: Dancer Tying Her Shoe *(c. 1880). Pastel (18³/₈ × 22⁷/₈ in.). Private Collection, U.S.*

132

Seated Figure of a Woman

I did this pastel in 1979. It is a portrait of one of my former colleagues, Fulvia. We made an agreement that if she would sit for ten drawings, I would let her keep one.

She posed during our lunch-hour break. I set up my office like a real studio. I took one of the armchairs from the waiting room, while my colleague quickly changed and assumed her pose. Then, I put up a big sheet of paper on the door to the office, which I wedged shut with a piece of wood. Everything was done like a film running at fast speed. The background of my office was completely camouflaged.

The drawing was done with wax-based pastel pencils, except for the background, which was covered with a chalk-based pastel and then sprayed with fixative.

For the flesh tones, I took advantage of the background color, lightening it in some places with hatching of yellow ocher. In the area that received the most light, I used white. For the fingertips, cheekbones, and nose, which should be a little warmer than the rest of the skin tones, I used vermilion red. I also used it to give a sense of volume and relief to the drawing. In the darker and therefore cooler parts, I used several shades of blue, ranging from ultramarine, in the very darkest areas, to a cerulean blue.

The head is shaded with sepia and cerulean pastels. Note, too, how the features of the face are not drawn in detail, but rather suggested through variations of tonality in the different planes of color, giving the impression of eyes, nose, and mouth.

I worked out the red dress, using hatching for its construction and superimposing tones of pink and blue, for example, for the shadows of the knee, the stomach, and the shoulder on the left.

I colored in the chair with black, smudged with a finger and then hatched over with the same pastel.

Finally I filled in the highlights, using the flat side of a white pastel around only half the figure to give it more depth.

Sometimes a pleasing effect can be obtained by leaving a pastel unfinished, skipping over a few details, which is something all artists do from time to time.

In this case I left the legs of the chair uncompleted. This method has always been used by the artists: if a work is balanced in tone before it is "finished," it is often best to leave it as it is.

A Notebook of Pastel Sketches

Another interesting quality of working with pastels (like watercolors) is the possibility to do very small sketches easily. The necessary equipment is very portable and not at all cumbersome.

Such sketches or notes are a help later, when doing larger works. Artists have always tried to give their final works the freshness of their notes. The most successful were the great masters, because their notes were immediate, lively, and had a sense of volume. Because a limited range of colors restricted the artists, they had to choose their tones carefully to convey the emotion they wanted.

Two Sketches by Vincent van Gogh

Van Gogh signed his paintings with only his first name, Vincent, and this is what his fellow painters called him. At the beginning of his career as an artist he was not particularly drawn to Impressionism. In fact, he wrote to his sister:

One hears a lot of talk about the Impressionists, one expects who knows what, and then... seeing their paintings for the first time, one is quite disillusioned. They seem ugly, rough and badly painted, badly drawn,

135

badly colored, quite wretched. This was my first impression when I arrived in Paris...

This impression was clearly a result of van Gogh's early artistic training. But he quickly changed his mind and embraced the new movement with the ardor and dedication we all know. Théo, his brother, a brilliant art dealer, blessed with excellent judgment and tastes, was among the first to seek out new talents among the Impressionists, handling works by Monet, Sisley, Pissarro, Gauguin, and Toulouse-Lautrec. He introduced van Gogh to Pissarro, who took to him immediately. Pissarro was convinced his friend would either go mad or would move beyond Impressionism.

Van Gogh, who did nothing with moderation, fulfilled both predictions. When they met, van Gogh was painting with a palette consisting mostly of dark tones, but when Pissarro explained the theory and techniques of Impressionism to him he became fascinated. He subsenquently followed these new ideas with enthusiasm.

In November 1885, van Gogh made the two sketches reproduced here, drawn on sketch paper taken from a horizontal notebook. I suggest you also try using a notebook in a small format like van Gogh

Vincent van Gogh: above, Salon with Women Dancing *(1885). Below,* Two Women in a Theatre Box *(1885). Pastels ($3^1/_2 \times 6^1/_4$ in.). Rijksmuseum Vincent van Gogh, Amsterdam.*

($6\text{-}^1/_2 \times 3\text{-}^1/_2$ inches). Note the rapidness of execution one can "read" in the strokes of these sketches. The black pastel and colored pencils seem to have been used almost simultaneously; the few lines show quite an extraordinary imagination.

The truly innovative artists who have left their mark on the history of art had, among their other qualities, an ability to invent new techniques that were daring, imaginative, and expressive. Van Gogh, who substituted for his lack of academic training with an enormous capacity for expression, was one of them.

Why don't you copy one of van Gogh's notes on a sheet of white paper and fill in the rest of the drawing, trying to imagine what he would have done? You will notice that every single little sketch is so full of emotion that it can be enlarged to become a composition in itself. These are the things that Action Painters observe most and take into consideration in their works.

Pages from a Picasso Notebook

The same year, 1901, in which Toulouse-Lautrec died, destroyed by alcohol, Vollard, an art dealer, held the first exhibition of works by a young Spanish artist who had been greatly influenced by Toulouse-Lautrec. His name was Pablo Picasso.

At sixteen, Picasso had written to a friend in Barcelona:

If I had a son who wanted to be a painter, I would not make him stay in Spain for a minute. And I do not think I would send him to Paris (where I would go quite willingly) but to Munik (I do not know if that is how it is spelled). It is a city where painting is studied seriously, without paying attention to styles like Pointillism *or whatever (I would not mind these styles if it were not that, once someone has invented something, everyone else copies it). I am not in favor of any particular school because they do nothing but produce a uniform group of followers.*

Picasso, however, quickly forgot about Munich when he went to Paris. There he spent his time studying Toulouse-Lautrec and Cézanne.

The influence of the Impressionists did not end with their death. It continued with Picasso, Matisse, and others, who picked up the flame and carried it on.

Turn to the next pages and look at these lovely Picasso sketches from 1900. The little figures sketched in the style of Degas, Toulouse-Lautrec, or Zandomeneghi seem

like snapshots—though in fact, photographers learned to frame their pictures like artists and not viceversa.

From this sketchbook, we see that Picasso not only created a "school" for himself, but he selected whom he wanted as teachers. He tried to assimilate as much as he could from the Impressionists before creating his own very personal style of art.

Two of these female figures are strongly outlined in black pastel, heavily emphasized with other color pastels, and then gone over again with black. You can actually see where the black pastel has been drawn over the other colors, instead of the opposite.

If you attempt to copy the technique used in these drawings, you will experience something of what the artists who did them felt. The common bond among them was their devotion to their work and this helped them carry on in spite of the obstacles they faced.

In this same period, Picasso did another pastel reproduced here which was not among the sketches in his notebook. It shows a completely new technique.

This pastel, a rather daring composition, is a good example of Picasso's approach to his work. He experimented with a wide range of methods and materials and looked

at each new work as if it were the first one he had ever done.

The picture is called *In the Dressing Room*.

Pablo Picasso: facing page, Parisian Woman, *from his notebook (1900). Pastel ($4^1/_8 \times 2^3/_8$ in.). This page, left,* Parisian Seamstress, *from his notebook. Pastel ($4^1/_8 \times 2^3/_8$ in.). Below,* In the Dressing Room, *(1900). Pastel ($18^7/_8 \times 20^7/_8$ in.). Museo Picasso, Barcelona.*

It was drawn on a very rough material, and it is likely that in certain places color was lightly rubbed on with a piece of very fine sandpaper. He then used this as a color base and continued with traditional techniques. However, it is hard to be sure just which techniques he used, since he experimented so much.

Picasso's pastel drawings suggest another important aspect of figure drawing that we should pay attention to—the setting in which the figure is placed.

Degas and the Figure in its Setting

Degas, perhaps because of his poor eyesight, could not work in bright light like the other Impressionists. He learned to make "photographs" in his mind of things he saw. Sitting in a bar, he would imprint a scene on his visual memory. The result was to create the illusion of a third dimension. Looking at one of his works, one can almost feel present in it.

I have chosen this particular pastel on the right for the range of colors Degas used, which I want to explain to you. Keep this book open at page 141 with the Degas's drawing, and try to reproduce on a sheet of paper the pastel colors he used.

Degas worked equally well with pastels, oil paints and pencil. During his last years, when he had almost completely lost his sight, he began sculpting. He made his model casts in clay and his statues in terracotta, or with the lost wax process. In this way, his fingers continued to express what he could no longer paint or draw.

Ingres, his idol, had been demanding in his days, and Degas judged others just as severely. Degas was a bit more indulgent with his followers, but his successor did not rise from among them. He was Henri de Toulouse-Lautrec, the friend of Degas's friend, Zandomeneghi.

The Salon in the Rue des Moulins by Toulouse-Lautrec

A pastel picture and an oil painting by Toulouse-Lautrec appear on pages 142 and 143. Look at the difference between the two. See how much fresher and more luminous the pastel looks.

Toulouse-Lautrec also used two different color schemes in these pictures. The woman in the foreground of the pastel is wearing black stockings, while the same woman in the oil painting is wearing greenish ones. The woman just behind her, in the pastel,

Edgar Degas: Women at a Café Terrace. *Pastel (16¹/₈×20⁵/₈ in.). Louvre, Paris.*

with her hands in her lap, is wearing a white dress instead of a violet one. The woman in the background on the left has on a gray outfit in one and black in the other. The divan and cushions are also different. But the biggest difference is that the execution of the pastel is much simpler than that of the oil painting.

Toulouse-Lautrec had learned from Degas and Zandomeneghi to compose his pictures like candid snapshots. Like Degas, Toulouse-Lautrec can make you feel as if you were part of the scene, almost as though you were looking over the artist's shoulder.

He found many of his models among the actors and actresses, dancers, and prostitutes around him. Toulouse-Lautrec immortalized them just as the princes and kings of the Renaissance had been immortalized by the artists of their time. What a clear example of how the subjects depicted in art have changed over the centuries.

The quest to capture ever more evocative moments led Toulouse-Lautrec to make quick sketches. This one is dense with color. The figures gradually begin to thin out as the eye moves back toward the central column. The column itself seems to be there more to give consistency to the figures than to be a structural component of the room.

A small, long-suffering man, Toulouse-Lautrec was beloved by his friends, who found him likable, open, and kind. From the faces of his subjects, we get a strong sense of what the artist was feeling. His art indicates the coming of Expressionism.

Henri de Toulouse-Lautrec: The Salon in Rue des Moulins *(1894). Oil painting (43^7/$_8$×52^1/$_8$ in.). Musée Toulouse-Lautrec, Albi.*

Henry de Toulouse-Lautrec: The Salon in Rue des Moulins *(1894). Pastel (51¹/₄×43³/₈ in.). Musée Toulouse-Lautrec, Albi.*

THE LANDSCAPE

Pastel landscapes are true displays of virtuosity. It is not easy to find an artist with many pastels of this kind in his collection, and Federico Zandomeneghi was one of the few important artists to create landscapes in pastels.

Federico Zandomeneghi: Landscape with Trees. *Pastel (19⁵/₈ × 23⁵/₈ in.). Private Collection, Milan.*

To draw a landscape, you must know the basic rules of construction, that is of perspective. Make your first, few drawings on grid paper, always sticking to a small format. The paper does not have to be of very high quality. An ordinary notebook will do very well for this purpose.

Use the little squares as reference points for your constructions. For example, if you were facing a house straight on, it might look like this (fig. 1).

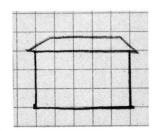

1

You could draw in the horizon line here (fig. 2).

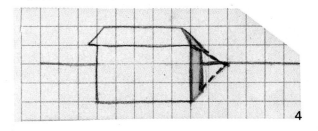

2

In the theory of perspective, the point at which receding parallel lines appear to meet is called the vanishing point (fig. 3).

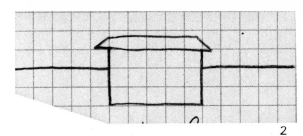

3

Now if you were to move a little to one side of the house, you would see it from a different angle (fig. 4).

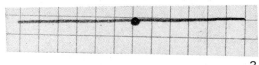

4

145

If you looked at it from a point slightly below the house, it would look like this (fig. 5), and would have two vanishing points.

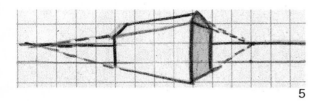

5

Try this simple exercise. Draw a landscape on grid paper, like the one below, which I have done using different colors for the different stages.

Remember, the shadows must be done correctly, too. Look at the part I did in blue.

Now, let us move on to a slightly more difficult exercise, again using the grid paper and small format. The sketch reproduced here was done in a very simple way to show you how to tackle more difficult compositions in stages.

Try to diagram it yourself, coloring it with flat colors as I have done in the drawing that you can see on the next page. This is a very good exercise for beginners; it teaches you how different colors can be used to create an illusion of depth, even when they are of the same tones. Look at the different greens,

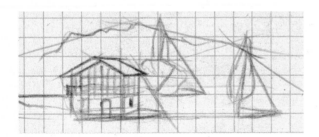

for example, and see how they become darker and bluer as they move toward the background.

Even if this exercise seems a bit trivial, it will help you see the different planes and surfaces. Go outside and do several of these sketches in your notebook, and later, when you are back inside, repeat them time and again, drawing only the essential elements and choosing each of the colors you use carefully.

Later, by referring to your notes, you can enlarge the drawing as much as you like—doubling or even tripling it in size. This is how the great artists were able to produce large-scale works starting from much smaller sketches.

View of London by Claude Monet

Monet led a rebellious adolescence. Ironically, even though he constantly skipped school, one of his great pleasure was to fill his notebooks with irreverent caricatures of his teachers.

He was a very capable caricaturist, so good, in fact, that by fifteen, he was receiving constant requests for his work. He earned 20 francs a piece for his pictures, which he displayed in the windows of a framer's shop in Le Havre, where he lived.

Through the frame-maker, Monet met Eugène Boudin, who introduced him to painting and steered him toward the idea of doing landscapes.

At seventeen, Monet had found an excellent teacher. No theorist, Boudin painted only what he saw. He taught his young student first to appreciate nature and only then to begin painting it. Boudin had often said to Monet:

You will never do it all by yourself unless you have a very strong character, and even then... art is not invented in solitude in some corner of the province...

The young Impressionists were often devoted to their teachers and both admired and had great esteem for each other. They

Claude Monet (1830-1926): View of London. *Pastel (11⁵/₈×17¹/₂ in.). Private Collection, Paris.*

believed themselves to be the elect of art, trading theories and ideas as well as making sacrifices for each other.

If one was successful, he would share the fruits of his success with his needier friends. In those days, there was respect and real generosity among colleagues. How things have changed in the art world today!

This pastel was done by Monet on one of the many trips he made to London between 1900 and 1903.

During these years, Monet's quest to capture the effects of light intensified. His fog is full of color, depth, and melancholy, yet he rendered it with only a few colors, bringing the background in toward the foreground and shading the colors with his finger.

You might try copying this pastel yourself, using pastel chalk and attempting to imitate his colors. Then, using Monet's techniques, you can move on to a landscape of your own.

Choose your landscape and, with your book in hand, study it; then try to draw it as you imagine Monet would have.

Remember to keep your eye constantly on the landscape as you draw and choose the colors closest to the ones you see. Develop the habit of observing things carefully be-fore you put anything on paper. The result should be a combination of what you see and what you feel inside.

Learn what you can from the masters with humility. It is the only way to receive and, in turn, give of yourself. Art is like the sea; each wave, like a picture, is endlessly followed by another and another. This is how you must execute your drawings, first one and then another and another, and so on, as you strive for perfection.

On a Beach near the Sea by Edgar Degas

Degas, a painter whose high viewpoints were later imitated by photographers, a painter of horses and dancers, and a pastelist by necessity, was also a great landscape artist. With three little boats, two tones of gray-blue, and four small, dark points on the sand, he created a miracle, which has been reproduced on the following page.

Its beauty lies in the way it is pared down to the bare essentials. Degas succeeded in reducing what we see to the minimum for the maximum effect.

Learning to recognize and select only the essential elements is not difficult. Look at your subject with half-closed eyes, imprint-

Edgar Degas: On a Beach near the Sea *(c. 1869). Pastel (11³/₄ × 18¹/₈ in.). Louvre, Paris.*

ing it in your mind, and draw everything that you can remember about it. Now go back and look at it again, memorize it again, and again draw what you remember. Degas's drawing seems to be such a visual memory. It is like the lakeshore cottage where one once spent a summer vacation. Though it was never seen again, it stays in the mind's eye forever.

When first doing landscapes, we are naturally drawn to reproduce details. My beginning students always start out drawing every shingle on a house or every leaf on a tree—all at the expense of the house's perspective or the tree's shape. But they soon learn to concentrate first of all on the shapes and understand that the details will emerge through the apt use and superimposition of colors.

Next time you go to a museum or exhibition, look closely at the works of the great masters. You will discover that even the Flemish artists did not go into great detail.

Returning to the Degas pastel, you might note a similarity to the Monet we just saw.

Degas, in this work, used his fingers to spread the pastels, smudging some colors and accentuating others with strong clean lines.

View of the Port of Honfleur
by Eugène Boudin

At the age of twenty, Boudin opened a stationery and framing store in Le Havre. It became a popular place for young painters to shop for supplies. Among these artists was Jean-François Millet, who at that time was still unknown.

One day Boudin visited Millet with some of his drawings and asked for his advice. No one knows exactly what Millet said, but immediately afterward, Boudin took up art very seriously.

Among his favorite subjects were the port and estuary of his native city, Honfleur.

In his view of the port, on the following page, Boudin, like the others, draw only the essential elements. He shaded the white-gray clouds with his finger on an azure-blue background of sky. The sea, a bit rough near the horizon, is done in indigo blue, while the water in the port has a slightly grayer tone than the sky. To achieve this effect, Boudin took advantage of the natural color of the paper.

This is still a figurative work from the 19th century. In the 20th century, abstract art was born, and pastels came to occupy a very special place.

Eugène Boudin (1824-1898): View of Port of Honfleur. *Pastel (8⁵/₈×11 in.). Private Collection, Paris.*

ABSTRACT ART

Artists have always tried to give the subjects of their portraits a soul, as if to make them speak. In the past, they tried to do this by capturing exactly the features of their subjects. Modern artists, however, do not see this as sufficient. Today they try to dig deeper into their subjects, to see what is beneath the surface, searching for a soul.

To help you understand the ideas of abstract art I will give you a simple example.

Every word is made up of letters which have specific sounds, and when they are put in a certain order, they have a particular meaning. If you change their order, you change their meaning.

Take, for example, the word *team* and assign each letter a different color. Thus T = red, E = yellow, A = gray, and M = blue. It forms this sequence: red, yellow, gray, blue. Now if you make a new word with the same letters, for example, *mate*, you would get the following color sequence: blue, gray, red, yellow.

If the subject interests you, you might like to read more on it. A very simple treatment of it can be found in *Theory of Form and Representation* by Paul Klee or *Point, Line and Surface* by Vassily Kandinsky.

An Abstract Pastel by Willem de Kooning

Willem de Kooning, a naturalized American artist, was born in Rotterdam in 1904. Because of financial difficulties, he was forced to leave school at the age of twelve. He attended night classes at the Rotterdam School of Art and eventually emigrated to the United States in 1926. He did his first abstract work in 1928, though later he tended to alternate between abstract and figurative art. There are in his work clear traces of such artists as Joan Miró and Jean Lurçat, as well as of Mexican Social Realism.

Between 1935 and 1945, he created a series of large "classic" figures of men and women. The latter were violently deformed with vehement, tormented gestures in the Expressionist tradition, which gave them a grotesque and sinister aspect. (*Men*, 1935-40, *Women*, first series, 1938-45). De Kooning's work played a key-role in the develop-

ment of contemporary American art by bringing certain European influences to the New World. They seem to attempt to sum up contemporary expression while continuing to use traditional materials and technical instruments. His first exhibition in 1948 brought him recognition as one of the leaders of the new school of young American artists, which included Jackson Pollock, Barnett Newmann, Mark Rothko, and Franz Kline, among others. In 1955 he began to produce a series of abstract landscapes (his other basic theme), which along with the human figure, evoke the misery and violence of urban American life.

Abstract Pastel by Nena Airoldi

In abstract art, strange techniques can be combined in very subjective and experimental ways that would make a Renaissance artist shudder. But what is important is the finished product and not how it was achieved.

The pastel reproduced on the right was made in 1964 by the sculptor Nena Airoldi, on tracing paper, sprayed with fixative sev-

Willem de Kooning: Woman *(c. 1952). Pastel (30×22 in.). Museum of Modern Art, New York.*

Nena Airoldi: Abstract Pastel *(1964). Pastel (27^1/$_2$×19^3/$_4$ in.). Collection of the Artist.*

eral times, and then placed on Japanese rice paper. The transparency of the tracing paper is maintained even with the superimposition of the pastels, and the effect achieved is remarkable.

I met Nena Airoldi around 1968. At that time she was searching for pure form in her art. Her sculptures were as harmonious and fluid as the movements of a cat. Each curve ran into another, suggesting beautiful imaginary spaces.

The pastel reproduced on the preceding page is a study done for a sculpture. Note that the white line, which moves along an almost spiral course on a pink background, was made by holding the pastel crayon flat. This creates a feeling of vibration that accentuates the movement of the white line. The orange circle on the violet background acts as a support (like a runner's feet) to the white line which ends in two blue shapes. The blue shapes are an optical counterweight to the orange circle. In fact, the blue, wedge-like shape, at the end of the white line, could be compared to the pole in a balancing act.

Taken as a whole, the composition suggests equilibrium and rhythm. If the drawing were turned into a sculpture, it could be made to turn, but it would always go back to where it had started, in perfect balance.

Abstract art is an expression of emotions, and it can be compared to poetry and the rhythm of its verses. This occurred to me after reading this poem by Vico Faggi, written after seeing a painting by Cézanne.

From a Cézanne

A cylinder. A sphere. A beautiful color.
The Cézanne apple.
On the glass of the fruit bowl.
It is perfect. Lucid. Fleeting.

Peace splinters
Into chips. Behind
The curtains a light like honey
Grows dirty. Clouds over. Night
Falls. Worry
Tightens its grip.

Those beacons, those ships,
Where do they go.

(Fuga dei Versi, Garzanti, Milan, 1986)

PASTELS AND WATERCOLORS

I often use water-soluble pastels for small, quick sketches like the one I have repro- duced here. They are very practical and easy to use—you simply work with them like nor-

mal pastels, superimposing one color on another. Then, with a wet brush, wash over your drawing. The colors will spread and create an effect like that of watercolors.

Once the colors have been superimposed and mixed with water you might find that the resulting effect is not correct. It's quite easy to solve this problem: spray some fixative over the wrong parts and then go over them with some new color, spreading it with a wet brush.

This technique can also be used for more demanding work such as illustrations for books and advertising.

Keep in mind when you use this technique that the paper on which you are working will get wet, and when it dries, it will tend to buckle. Therefore, it is best to prepare it as if you were painting a watercolor.

Dip the paper in water until it is thoroughly wet. Then, take it out of the water, and with a small, stiff brush, spread a thin strip of glue around the four edges. Place the glued side of the paper down on a board slightly larger than your paper and smooth it out. Once it has dried you may begin to work. If you prepare your paper this way,

you will avoid unpleasant surprises. In fact, after this treatment, even if you soak the paper completely as you work, if will stay flat when it dries again.

Of course, if you prefer, you can also use paper made for watercolors. In that case, look for the kind with a rough grain.

Using pastels this way offers you a whole new range of techniques to explore. You can achieve different effects according to the kind of brush you use. Try a stiff bristle with a flat point or a very soft sable brush or even a wad of cotton attached to a short stick. I invite you to try out this technique in as many ways as possible. I assure you it will not fail to surprise you with the possibilities it offers.

Another use for water-soluble pastels is as a part of a mixed technique, for example, to go over tempera or colored pastels.

They are also often used by illustrators to add special effects to their drawings.

One last suggestion. When you sharpen your water-soluble pastels, save the shavings in a small container. When you have accumulated enough, add a little water to them and use them with your pastels to give extra depth to a color.

INDEX